The Seerah of the Final Prophet

Peace & Blessings Be Upon Him

Hasan Al-Banna

Awakening Publications

Published by
Awakening Publications
Uplands Business Centre
Bernard Street
Swansea
SA2 0DR

Author: Hasan Al-Banna

British Library Cataloguing in Publication Data
Al-Banna, Hasan
The Seerah of the Final Prophet
1. Islam
I. Title

Cover Design: Wali-ur Rahman

Typeset: Razia Akhtar Fatima
Printed and bound by Deluxe Printers, London NW10 7NR
Telephone: 0208 965 1771

Dedicated...

To my beloved parents who brought me up learning to read and write
and to those future leaders of the Islamic Movement in the West.

CONTENTS

From the Author's Father   13
Foreword   14
Preface   16
Eulogy   19
Author's Preface   20

INTRODUCTION
From Prophet Ibrahim to Prophet Muhammad   28
Map of Arabia and the Middle East   29
Arabia Before Islam   30
Abdul Muttalib and Abdullah   35
The Year of the Elephant   37

BIRTH OF MUHAMMAD
Infancy   40
Childhood   42
Life as a Shepherd   43
Expedition to Syria   43

LIFE AS A YOUTH
Battle of Fujjar and Hilful Fudhul   45
Trading Expeditions   46
Marriage to Khadijah   47
Ka'bah and its Rebuilding   48
Craving for the Truth   49
Qur'an is Revealed   51
Khadijah and Waraqa Ibn Nawfal   52

THE MISSION AND THE MOVEMENT

Stage of Secret Da'wah 55
Ali Ibn Abu Talib Enters Islam 56
Abu Bakr Enters Islam 57
The First Muslims 58
Stage of Open Da'wah 60
Reaction to the Da'wah 64

RIDICULE AND PROPAGANDA

Attempts at Compromise 68
Persecution of the Believers 72
Rule of Makkah is Offered 74
Migration to Abyssinia 76
Hamza Ibn Abdul Muttalib Accepts Islam 79
Umar Ibn Al Khattab Accepts Islam 80
Social and Economic Boycott 83
Death of Abu Talib 84
Death of Khadijah 86
Prophet is Unprotected 87
Mission to Taif 89

MI'RAJ: THE PROPHET MEETS ALLAH

Salah: Mi'raj of the Believers 96
Abu Bakr is Al Siddiq 97
Da'wah in Yathrib 99
The First Aqabah 100
The Second Aqabah 101

HIJRAH: MIGRATION TO MADINAH

Attempts to Capture the Prophet 107

Arrival at Quba   110
Reception at Yathrib   111
Mosque: Centre of the Islamic Society   112
As Sahifah: First Constitution of the World   114

ESTABLISHMENT OF THE FIRST ISLAMIC STATE

The Islamic Brotherhood   118
Establishment of Salah   121
Adhan: The Call to Prayer   122
Change of the Qiblah   123
Betrayal by the Jews   125
Emergence of Hypocrites   128
The Obligation of Zakah   128
Fast of Ramadhan is Enjoined   129
Early Conditions of the Muslims   130
Public Treasury is Established   131

JIHAD: STRUGGLE IN THE WAY OF ALLAH

Events Leading up to Badr   133
Preparations for War   135

BATTLE OF BADR

Prisoners of War   140
In-between Badr and Uhud   142

BATTLE OF UHUD

Victory then Defeat   147
Quraish Mutilate the Dead   149
After the Battle   150
Banu Asad Plan to Attack Madinah   152

The Three Martyrs 153
Banu Nadir's Plot to Kill the Prophet 155
The Second Badr 158

BATTLE OF THE TRENCH
Jews Conspire with the Quraish 161
Digging the Trench 162
Banu Qurayza are Persuaded 165
The Faith of the Muslims is Tested 166
Nuyam's Plot to Defeat the Quraish 167
The Storm and the Retreat of the Quraish 168
Siege of Banu Qurayza 169
Banu Al Mustaliq 171
Case of Tuama and the Jew 171

THE TREATY OF HUDAYBIYA
Muslims Go to Makkah 174
Urwa Ibn Mas'ud 175
Uthman Ibn Affan is Sent to the Quraish 177
Treaty is Accepted 178
Invitations to Islam 181
Banu Khaybar are Besieged 183
Downfall of the Jews 185
Muslims Go to Makkah for Umrah 186
Harith Ibn Umayr is Killed 187

BATTLE OF MUTA
Khalid IbnWalid - Sword of Allah 189
The Hudaybiya Treaty is Violated 191
Abu Sufyan Goes to Madinah 192

The March Towards Makkah   194
Abu Sufyan Enters Islam   197

THE CONQUEST OF MAKKAH
The Quraish are Forgiven   199
The Ansars are Worried   201
Quraish Accept Islam   201

BATTLE OF HUNAYN
Siege of Taif   205
Shaima: The Prophet's Foster Sister   206
Distribution of the Booty   207
Spread of Islam   207
Banu Tamim Enters Islam   208
Deputation from Arab Tribes   208

CAMPAIGN OF TABUK
The Muslims are Tested   211
March Towards Tabuk   214
The Romans Retreat   215
Treaties are Signed   215
Potential Murderers are Forgiven   216
Three Men are Forgiven by Allah   217
Types of Men the Prophet Dealt With   217
The Mosque of the Hypocrites   219
Angel of Death Visits Abdullah Ibn Ubayy   220

THE YEAR OF DELEGATIONS
Urwa Ibn Masud Embraces Islam   222
Deputation from Taif   223

Abu Bakr Leads the Pilgrimage   225
The Prophet's Last Pilgrimage   226

THE FAREWELL SPEECH
The Last Revelation   231
False Prophets   232
Preparations Against Rome   234

THE PROPHET FALLS ILL
The Prophet Visits the Graves   235
Relationship with Abu Bakr   236
Fatimah Cries, Fatimah Laughs   238
The Prophet Wishes to Write   238
Disposing the Seven Dinars   239

THE PROPHET PASSES AWAY
Muslims are Shocked   241
Reaction of Umar Ibn Al Khattab   241
Reaction of Abu Bakr   242

ABU BAKR BECOMES KHALIFAH
Burial of the Prophet   245

Afterword   247
Seerah at a Glance   249
Collection of non-Muslim Verdicts on Prophet   253
Letters Sent by the Prophet   258
Selected References   260

From the Author's Father

All praises are due to Allah and may peace and blessings of Allah be upon our Final Prophet Muhammad.

I express my sincere love and devotion for the Final Messenger of Allah - Muhammad, peace and blessings be upon him, and for his revolutionary companions who changed the course of history. I also express my love for those, who throughout the centuries, have striven for the revival of Islam; especially the founder of the Islamic Movement in the twentieth century and of the Al-Ikhwan Al Muslimoon - Egypt's Shaheed Imam Hasan Al-Banna (*rahimahullah*). It is solely based on my love and admiration for him that I have named my son Hasan Al-Banna, who I give to the Islamic revival as a *waqf*.

I pray that Allah enables him to be a correct follower of the Final Prophet Muhammad (peace and blessings of Allah be upon him) and that through him the uncompleted work of Shaheed Imam Hasan Al-Banna is completed. May Allah give him the ability to strive for the propagation and revival of Islam in the West, as a successor of Imam Al-Banna. Ameen.

Maulana Muhammad Abdul Quadir
Founder Principal of Jamiatul Ummah (London)
& Madinatul Uloom (Bradford)
London, UK
September 1997

Foreword

I began reading the book on the Seerah of the Prophet Muhammad (peace and blessings of Allah be upon him) to write a foreword, but I found that it was quite necessary for me to read it for learning as well. The life of the Prophet Muhammad (peace and blessings of Allah be upon him) and his seerah is a very rich resource for all generations at all times and places. No one book can be the only authentic book about this topic. This book, which is written by a young Muslim who is a non-Arab, is an indication of the global phenomena of the Deen of Islam and is an indication of the universality of the mission of the Prophet Muhammad (peace and blessings of Allah be upon him):

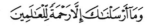

And We have not sent you but as a mercy for mankind.
(s21 : v107)

The Seerah of the Prophet Muhammad (peace and blessings of Allah be upon him) and the various aspects, situations and events characterising his life, made his life an open book for Muslims and non-Muslims to read, benefit from and think about. There is nothing to hide about the life of the Prophet (peace and blessings of Allah be upon him); even the relationship with his wives is an example to be followed. His life is the example and model in our day to day living; example and model in times of peace and war; example and model in writing to and inviting kings and emperors and the example and model in the domestic as well as the foreign policy of a state:

لَّقَدْ كَانَ لَكُمْ فِى رَسُولِ ٱللَّهِ أُسْوَةٌ حَسَنَةٌ

Indeed in the Messenger of Allah you have a good example to follow.
(s33 : v21)

I wish all the best for brother Hasan Al Banna and hope to see more of his production in the field of Uloom ul Qur'an and Uloom ul Hadith and other Islamic Sciences. Now that Hasan Al Banna speaks Arabic, we hope for a new scholar in the West, in the likes of Ibn Hazm, who was from Andalus (Spain) and Imam Al Bukhari (Bukhara) and other great scholars of Islam who were not Arabs, but millions of Arabs learnt from them. This is one of the aspects of the sweetness and secrets of Islam and the Arabic language.

Let us hope for a good number of scholars who are born and raised in the West and who can be good models for Islam in the West.

Dr. Kamal Helbawy
President of Muslim Association of Britain
London, UK
March 1998

Preface

For the 1.5 billion Muslims around the globe, the Last Prophet Muhammad (peace and blessings of Allah be upon him) is the central personality. Everyday in everything, even in the most intimate personal deeds in the life of a believer, the life of the Prophet is referred to. His examples, his words and some actions of some of his associates (may Allah be pleased with them) which were approved by him, are the point of reference for every Muslim.

The hadith literature are the first category of the above, compiled in a way that a Muslim can refer to with ease and derive guidance for everyday life, from simple personal matters of eating, drinking etc. to the more critical matters of the Ummah and the State. They are not written chronologically, but subject-wise, covering every aspect of the life of the Prophet, from articles of faith to the rules of Jihad (struggle for the emancipation of humanity) to international relations, and inevitable events beyond this world.

From Ibn Ishaq onward, the present style of chronological order in writing the Seerah (i.e from the Prophet's birth to his departure from this world) started developing. There is no survey available as to how many books in different languages have been written so far about the life of the Noble Prophet. In every language spoken by the Muslims there are many treatises on the life of the Prophet. Even non-Muslims wrote on his life. Some of the Western writers tried intentionally to distort facts and present him as the original founder of the Islamic religion. But there are others who are sincere writers; among them is Professor Ramakrishna Rao and the German translator Guilleme who took so much trouble to translate the Life of the Prophet by Ibn Hisham.

The approach to writing the Seerah varies from writer to writer. The approach in this book, has its origin in the commentary of the Qur'an by Sayyid Abul Ala Mawdudi. In his introduction to Surah Al An'am, Maulana Mawdudi has given some details. However, the process of social change followed by the Prophet under the Divine Guidance, has been one of the very important topics in the tarbiyyah system of the Islamic Movement. The Prophet's life in this approach is studied on the Qur'anic divide of Makkan and Madinan chapters. These chapters are subdivided into several stages and the gradual evolution of the Islamic Society is focused upon.

The Prophet of Islam during his life in Makkah organised some individuals, who in addition to basic human qualities developed the Islamic qualities of Iman, Taqwa, Sabr and Ihsan. They became the examples of the 'Walking Qur'an,' easily identifiable by their lifestyles. These were the people who later in the Islamic Society of Madinah provided leadership in every walk of life, including the role of Generals in great battles for the liberation of the vast number of human beings in the then Arabia and it's immediate neighbourhood.

This approach was first used by Maulana Abu Salim Abdul Hay (Rampur, India) in his book 'Hayat at Tayyibah' written within the four walls of a prison. Because he did not have access to source materials, he had to keep it to a minimum without many quotations or references. Greater use of this approach was later used by Safiur Rahman Al Mubarakpuri (Azamgori, India), a lecturer in the Islamic University of Madinah, in his book 'Ar Raheeq al

Makhtoom'. The approach received so much appreciation that in a competition held by Rabita Alam Al Islami, in Makkah in 1979, on the life of the Prophet; his book received the first prize.

The writer of the present book, my young brother Hasan Al Banna, the namesake of the founder and Murshid Al Aam of the great Islamic Movement Al Ikhwan Al Muslimoon, has followed the same approach. Some writers have tried to present the life of the Noble Prophet in a simple way for the young readers. To my limited knowledge this is a first attempt by a young Muslim to express his love and admiration of the Prophet for the young people of his age.

By including a good number of Qur'anic quotations and references, he will receive the appreciation of the senior youth, especially as it has become a trend these days to demand references on anything one says about Islam.

This is the first attempt of the present writer and I pray to Allah that he develops himself into a prolific writer as did Maulana Mawdudi (*rahimahullah*). The Ummah lacks prolific writers who can write on every aspect of our lives and contribute towards the upliftment of the Ummah through the development of human sciences within the constraint of a comprehensive Islam.

Muhammad Abdus Salam
Former President of UK Islamic Mission & Da'watul Islam UK & Eire
London, UK
September 1997

Eulogy

I have read Hasan Al Banna's book on the Seerah of the Final Prophet. Praise be to Allah, it is worthy of praise and his work is of a high standard.

Many writers have written on the Seerah resulting in the in-depth study of every aspect of the Prophet's life. However, this particular book has been written for the young generation of the modern world to introduce them to the Seerah. And I can confidently say that the author has been highly successful, from his part, in presenting the subject. He has dealt with the issues in a way comprehendable to his target audience. The style is simple and precise, yet inclusive of all the important events in the life of the Prophet Muhammad (peace and blessings of Allah be upon him).

I am confident that through the reading of this book, readers will receive a complete and authentic picture of the life of the Final Prophet.

Shaykh Muhammad Talha Bukhari
Darul Uloom, Deoband (*Fadhil* and *Takmeel Tafseer*)
Member of the European Council for Fatwa and Research
LLB (Magdah University, India)
BA (Magdah University, India)
MA Persian (University of Bahar, India)
MA Islamic Studies (Alighar Muslim University, India)
MA Arabic (Alighar Muslim University, India)

Author's Preface

And verily, for you are on an exalted standard of character[1]

And We have not sent you but as a Mercy to Mankind[2]

Thus spoke Allah, the Lord and Sustainer of the worlds, about our beloved Messenger and Final Prophet Muhammad (peace and blessings of Allah be upon him); a man whose teachings are being implemented even till today, in many aspects of human life. His life provides us with guidance for every single aspect of human life; ranging from minute personal matters, such as the cutting of nails or the manner of sitting and sleeping, to the more important aspects of society, such as the formulation of the foreign policy of the state. Whenever there has been an absence of the implementation of his teachings in society, individuals and movements arose in order to revive them; and such is the case today.

The teachings of Prophet Muhammad (peace and blessings of Allah be upon him) are being implemented today in the lifestyles of many Muslims around the globe, but only partially. Some aspects of his life are neglected, some are over-emphasised, some are given unnecessary priority over others and other aspects are completely misunderstood due to lack of correct knowledge and ignorance.

The Prophet was sent by Allah to liberate mankind from the

---

1. وَإِنَّكَ لَعَلَىٰ خُلُقٍ عَظِيمٍ   s68:v4

2. وَمَآ أَرْسَلْنَاكَ إِلَّا رَحْمَةً لِّلْعَالَمِينَ   s21:v107

20

worship of man-made idols and systems and provide mankind with guidance in order that they worship their Creator, Sustainer, Provider and the Lord of Mankind Allah. The Prophet was able to liberate the ignorant, illiterate and barbaric Arabs from the darkness of jahiliyyah to the light of Islam. The society in the Arabian Peninsula was completely transformed. A society that attached no importance to knowledge and in which most of its members were illiterate and ignorant was transformed into a society that produced scholars and intellectuals in every sphere of knowledge and human sciences, be it in the sciences of the Qur'an, Hadith, Fiqh or in Mathematics, Chemistry, Physics, Sociology, Geography etc. A society in which the poor and weak were oppressed was transformed into a society which became the flag-bearer of justice and equality. A society in which daughters were buried alive and in which women had no status, was transformed into a society which believed that Paradise lies at the feet of mothers. A society that fought long battles over petty issues such as the theft of a camel was transformed into a society that fought to uphold the ultimate Truth and eliminate Falsehood.

What lies in the reader's hand, is a modest attempt by the author on a lofty subject, on which countless books have been written. The author has tried to describe the life and the personality of the Final Messenger who transformed such a society and has not approached the subject in the spirit of an intellectual critic, but with a sincere love and humble devotion for his Prophet.

In writing this book, the author feels it has a number of characteristics which distinguish it from other books of Seerah. Certainly the final analysis is left to the readers:

1. Target Audience

Teenagers of the ages between 13 and 18. Many books have been written on the present subject, but to the present author's limited knowledge, there are very few books, if any, written on the Seerah which caters for this vital age group.

2. Simplicity of Expression

Many writers have written on the subject and the style of writing differs from writer to writer. Some writings are affected by the writer's intellectual and scholarly approach, such that the expression and style of writing reaches beyond the grasp of an average reader of the afore-mentioned age group. This has been avoided in the present book as the author feels that the comprehension of the subject by the readers is of more importance than the display of one's linguistic jargon. The fact that the present author began writing this book at the age of fifteen has helped tremendously in retaining the simplicity of expression for his readers (the original writing of this book was completed before the author had taken his GCSE exams).

3. Link between the Qur'an and the Seerah

Throughout this book, numerous verses of the Qur'an have been quoted (the Arabic text and the translation) in its relevant context, thus providing the readers with a conceptual link between the revelation of the Qur'an and the Seerah.

4. Approach to the Subject

Many approaches exist in writing the Seerah, ranging from the subject-based hadith literature to the chronological history of the Prophet's life. The present book approaches the subject in the latter manner with the additional feature of focusing on the mission of the Prophet. The phases of the Prophet's Islamic Movement have been outlined and analysis given as and when necessary.

5. Use of Arabic Terminologies

In order to familiarise the readers with certain important Islamic terminologies and concepts, in many places of the book the Arabic term for such terminologies and concepts have mentioned (i.e. *Iman, Risalah, Akhirah, Jahannam, Jannah, Tawheed, Shirk, Da'wah, Jama'ah, Tarbiyyah, Al Harakah Al Islamiyyah* etc.).

I owe a deep gratitude to my beloved and respected father Hafiz Maulana Muhammad Abdul Quadir. He has spent his entire life in the Islamic Movement working for the Islamic Revival and is currently the Principal of Jamiatul Ummah (the first movement orientated madrasah in Britain) and Ameer of Da'watul Islam UK and Eire (one of the senior organisations of the Islamic Movement in Britain). It is he who realised the need of a book on the Seerah aimed at teenagers in a simple and lucid style. He not only inspired me in writing this book, but instilled in me a love for the Final Messenger of Allah and guided me throughout the writing of the book. Many of the source materials in Arabic and Urdu were made available to me through his translations and explanations. Without his support, the writing of this book and its publication would not have been possible. I also owe gratitude to my beloved mother on whose lap I had learnt to read the Qur'an, which was revealed to the Prophet as guidance to mankind. In times when I felt that the task of writing the Seerah was difficult, her constant help and encouragement made it possible. May Allah reward them both for all their efforts.

I would like to extend my appreciation and thanks to Dr. Kamal Helbawy, Dr. Kadhim Al Rawi and Shaykh Bukhari for their help and valuable suggestions. Dr. Kadhim Al Rawi (one of the foremost Muslim Historians in Europe and a lecturer of Islamic History at the European Institute of Islamic Sciences in France) took the trouble of verifying the factual details of the book. Janab Muhammad Abdus Salam very kindly reviewed the manuscript and also gave some valuable suggestions. I am deeply obliged to him. Finally, I would like to thank all those brothers and sisters who tirelessly went through my book and made valuable comments and suggestions. May Allah reward them all.

If there is any merit to be found in this book, it is absolutely due to the Mercy of Allah, however, for any faults, the author is to be held responsible.

Hasan Al Banna
Bradford, UK
September 1997

INTRODUCTION

The human race began from one man Adam. It was from him that the family of man grew and the human race multiplied.

Adam, the first man on earth, was also the first Prophet of Allah. Allah revealed His religion: Islam, to him, so that he could explain to his people and teach them that - 'Allah is One. He is the Creator and the Sustainer of the world. He alone should be worshipped and from Him alone they should seek help. One day they will return to Him and they will be judged according to their conduct on earth: the righteous will be rewarded and the wrong-doers will be punished.'

When Prophet Adam conveyed his message to his children, those who were obedient followed and obeyed him knowing that this was the right path, but those who were evil disbelieved him and began to worship the sun, the moon, the stars whilst others began to worship trees, animals and rivers. Some even believed that air, water, fire, wind, health and all the other blessings were each under the control of different gods and thus each of them should be worshipped separately. In this way many religions began to form. Every nation made a different religion for itself and each one had their own god.

But the One Lord and Creator of mankind and of the universe was altogether forgotten. Not only that, even the people who used to obey Allah forgot the right path. Those things that were bad and evil were considered right and many good things were considered evil.

At this stage, Allah began to raise Prophets amongst every nation and people. The Prophets preached to their own people and tried their best to guide them to the right path. Some sources say 124,000 Prophets were sent to this earth. They included Prophets like Nuh, Ibrahim, Musa, Isa and Muhammad (peace and blessings of Allah be upon them all).

Each of the Prophets reminded the people of the lessons they had forgotten. They taught them to worship One God and tried to put an end to the worship of idols. God's Prophets were raised in all countries, in every land and amongst every people. They all preached the same message - the worship of One Allah *(Tawhid)*.

Prophet Nuh called his people to the truth for nine hundred and fifty years and achieved very little success. He was ignored, laughed at and mocked by his people. Nevertheless, those people were punished by a flood which killed them all. Only Prophet Nuh and his few followers along with two species from each sector of animal life were saved because they had built an ark in preparation for the punishment. Even his own son, who was a disbeliever, was killed in this flood.

Prophet Ibrahim plays a very important role in human history. He was brought up in an era when people were completely ignorant to the worship of One Allah. His people were living their lives for material things of the world. He was chosen by Allah to bring back the knowledge of Tawhid. He received fierce opposition from his people, even from his own father and had to leave his home. Once he was put into a fire, but Allah saved him from any harm. Prophet Ibrahim is considered the father of all monotheistic faiths.

Prophet Musa was also brought up in surroundings alien to Islam and the worship of One Allah. He had to encounter the Pharaoh of Egypt who was considered to be a god. He faced many obstacles and overcame them all with the Help of Allah. His life is an example as to how a superpower can be defeated.

Prophet Isa was also sent to the people of Bani Israil to revive and purify the teachings of Prophet Musa. He is not the founder of Christianity. Sources prove that Paul, who had never seen Prophet Isa (Jesus) invented the religion of Christianity. The fundamental change made to the original teachings of Prophet Isa was the addition of the concept of Trinity: 'Father, Son and Holy Ghost'. Other concepts such as 'original sin' were also added.

In Arabia, a Prophet was raised for the whole of mankind and not just for a particular group or nation as the previous Prophets were raised. The religion that he was given was again Islam. He was made a Prophet for the entire human race. His name was Muhammad Ibn Abdullah, the last and final Messenger of Allah. No other person in human history has left so deep faith (in God) on the life of his followers as Prophet Muhammad, Peace and Blessings of Allah be upon him. His life is the best example to follow.

It is part of the Islamic manners in showing respect to the Prophet to say 'Peace and Blessings of Allah be upon him' when his name is heard or read. Every reader is requested to abide by this manner while reading the book.

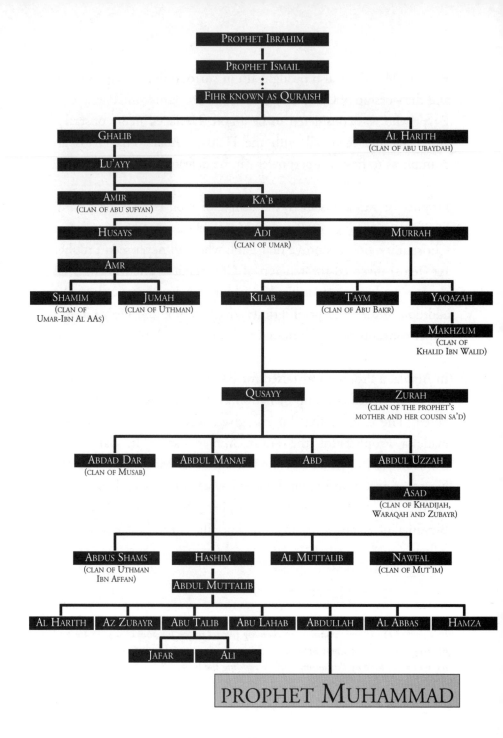

PROPHET IBRAHIM

PROPHET ISMAIL

FIHR KNOWN AS QURAISH

GHALIB

AL HARITH
(CLAN OF ABU UBAYDAH)

LU'AYY

AMIR
(CLAN OF ABU SUFYAN)

KA'B

HUSAYS

ADI
(CLAN OF UMAR)

MURRAH

AMR

SHAMIM
(CLAN OF
UMAR-IBN AL AAS)

JUMAH
(CLAN OF UTHMAN)

KILAB

TAYM
(CLAN OF ABU BAKR)

YAQAZAH

MAKHZUM
(CLAN OF
KHALID IBN WALID)

QUSAYY

ZURAH
(CLAN OF THE PROPHET'S
MOTHER AND HER COUSIN SA'D)

ABDAD DAR
(CLAN OF MUSAB)

ABDUL MANAF

ABD

ABDUL UZZAH

ASAD
(CLAN OF KHADIJAH,
WARAQAH AND ZUBAYR)

ABDUS SHAMS
(CLAN OF UTHMAN
IBN AFFAN)

HASHIM

AL MUTTALIB

NAWFAL
(CLAN OF MUT'IM)

ABDUL MUTTALIB

AL HARITH · AZ ZUBAYR · ABU TALIB · ABU LAHAB · ABDULLAH · AL ABBAS · HAMZA

JAFAR · ALI

PROPHET MUHAMMAD

28

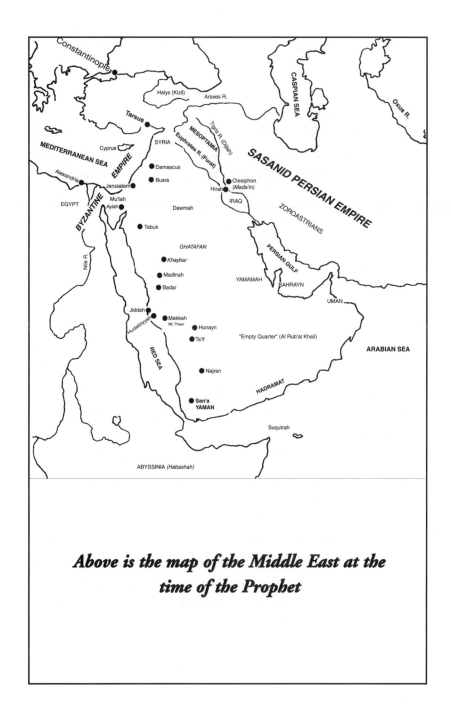

*Above is the map of the Middle East at the
time of the Prophet*

29

Arabia Before Islam

Arabia lies surrounded by the Red Sea on the west, by the Indian Ocean to the south, by the Persian Gulf in the east, and on the north by Syria. Over a third of its land is covered with sandy deserts, the hills barren and valleys consisting of dry beds. Except in the south-west, there are no rivers that flow the whole year round. The famous cities, Makkah and Madinah lie in Hijaz which extends along the Red Sea between Syria in the north and Yemen in the south.

It is in the city of Makkah that the Prophet Muhammad was to be born. Historically, this is the oldest of the cities in the world. It is also the city in which Hajera and Prophet Ismail; wife and son of Prophet Ibrahim, came at the command of Allah. As it happened, she was unable to find water for her son and started running between the mountains of Safa and Marwa in search of water. On returning back, she found there was a stream of clear water gushing from the ground beneath the feet of the child. This spring was afterwards known as Zam-Zam. In the heart of the city stands the Ka'bah, which was destroyed many times and was finally rebuilt by Prophet Ibrahim and Prophet Ismail.

Arabia was famous for its gold, silver and precious stones. The main produce was dates and of the animals found there, the most valuable was the camel - 'Ship of the Desert'. Their soil was poor and the main form of livelihood was either rearing camels, horses, cattle or they were engaged in the transportation of merchandise along the trading routes of the deserts.

The Arabs were children of the desert. As a result of their desert life, qualities of strength, endurance and quickness of temper were acquired. The Arabs were slow to forgive an injury and quarrels which would last for generations. One such example would suffice to understand the ethos prevailing in Arabia. Shanfara of Azd is a typical Arab hero. It is said that he was captured whilst a child, from his tribe by the Banu Salman, and brought up among them; he did not learn of his origin until he had grown up and vowed vengeance against his captors, and returned to his own tribe. His oath was that he would slay a hundred men of Banu Salman; he slew ninety-eight, when an ambush succeeded in taking him prisoner. In the struggle one of his hands was cut off by a sword stroke; taking the sword in the other hand he flung it across his enemy and killed him, making ninety-nine. Then he was overpowered and slain. As Shanfara's skull lay bleeding on the ground, a man from his enemies passed by and kicked it with his foot, a splinter of bone entered his foot, the wound mortified and he died, thus completing the hundred.

Contrasting the above qualities was the hospitable nature of the Arabs, which was to be found nowhere else in the world. They were brave, generous and loyal. Generosity was given such a status in society that if a stranger once sat to eat with them then they would consider it a duty to protect him. They would often kill their last sheep or goat to feed their guests. This hospitable nature could explain one of the reasons for Allah choosing the Arabs as the primary vehicle for transmitting the final message of Islam.

It was Prophet Ibrahim who first taught the Arabs the worship of One Allah (Tawhid) and started some of the ceremonies of pilgrimage to the Ka'bah. For a time, the desert Arabs followed the teachings of Prophet Ibrahim, but later began to deviate from the Straight Path; as was the case with all the followers of the Prophets. They started worshipping others besides Allah *(Shirk)*. Some of the tribes worshipped the stars, moon and sun; others made idols out of stone and a few were fire-worshippers. Thus the Ka'bah which was the centre of the worship of One Allah was transformed into a centre of idol worshipping. Within the Ka'bah itself, there were three hundred and sixty idols one for every day of the year. The greatest of these was Hubal. It was carved out of red granite, in the form of a man with the right hand broken off. The Arabs would name their children after the two famous idols, Abd Manah and Zayd Manah.

The Ka'bah was circumambulated by both men and women in a state of nudity with their hands clapping, shouting and singing and it was thought to be an act of piety. The justification given to such indecent acts was that it was unfair on their part to perform this sacred ceremony wearing the very clothes in which, they had committed sins. They would prostrate before the idols, give sacrifices and leave aside part of their produce and animals as offerings. Religious beliefs were founded on superstitions.

Although the Arabs worshipped idols, they did believe in the existence of one Great Deity. But at the same time believed the notion that the All Powerful had delegated His powers. Thus they had this misconception that the idols were merely a channel with which they could please Allah. The Qur'an testifies to this in the following ways:

وَلَئِن سَأَلْتَهُم مَّنْ خَلَقَهُمْ لَيَقُولُنَّ اللَّهُ فَأَنَّىٰ يُؤْفَكُونَ ۝

And if you ask them who created them,
they will surely say: "Allah". How then are they
turned away (from the worship of Allah).
(Az Zukhruf 43 : v 87)

وَلَئِن سَأَلْتَهُم مَّنْ خَلَقَ السَّمَٰوَٰتِ وَالْأَرْضَ لَيَقُولُنَّ خَلَقَهُنَّ الْعَزِيزُ الْعَلِيمُ ۝

And indeed if you ask them,
"Who has created the heavens and the
earth?" They will surely say: "The
All Mighty, the All Knower has created them."
(Az Zukhruf 43 : v 9)

The nomadic Arabs could not realise the stupidity of worshipping objects which they had created with their own hands. Once, a chief of a tribe went to the idols, intending to consult with it about taking revenge over his father's killing. When he received a negative reply drawing lots over and over again he retorted: "Wretched! You would not be answering 'no' if it were your father!"

The social and economic life of the Arabs presented no better picture. They were merely nomads wandering around with animals from place to place, and would set up tents wherever food and water was to be found. Drinking alcohol was an evil which had invaded all of Arabia. There was not a household which did not have a number of pitches in the store. The common social pastime was another social evil - gambling. Education was alien in the society. Very few people could read or write. Sayings of soothsayers and fortune tellers were believed and acted upon.

There was no central government, king or ruler of Arabia. However, certain tribes and figures tended to have more power and influence than others. They would exploit the masses mentally and economically. The economic system was based on interest. The usual method adopted for lending and then of its repayment was highly exploitative. Money was lent at high rates of interest, and when the money was not returned at its stipulated time, it was doubled and trebled at the expiry of the third year. In cases when the debtor failed to pay the loans, their wife and children were possessed. Speculation was too rampant on the rates of exchange. Even the Ka'bah was used as the centre of economic exploitation. Firstly, it was geographically in an important strategic position for business routes; thus taxes were levied on goods whilst going through Makkah and secondly, every year at the pilgrimage all the offerings, sacrifices of money, food and animals were collected at the Ka'bah. Thus it was only a minority which controlled and dictated society.

Women were treated as mere objects. Daughters were regarded as a disgrace and thus in many cases were buried alive. On the birth of a daughter, the family would be shocked. When a girl attained the age of six, the father would tell the child's mother to perfume and adorn the child with ornaments. He would then carry her to the wilderness; where a pit would be dug and the child would be made to stand by it. The father would then tell the child to focus her eyes on the pit and push her into it from behind. The ditch would be covered with clay and then levelled to the ground, burying his child alive. The Qur'an describes and condemns such prevailing attitudes in the following words:

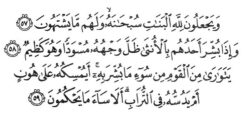

And they assign daughters unto Allah. Glorified be He above all that they associate with Him. And unto themselves what they desire. And when the news (of the birth) of a female is brought to any of them, his face becomes dark filled with inward grief. He hides himself from the people because of the evil of that whereof he has been informed. Shall he keep her with dishonour or bury her in the earth ? Certainly, evil is their decision.

(An Nahl 16 : v 57-59)

In cases where the daughters were not buried, they were turned into marketable commodities to be sold, bought and used. The married woman had no rights over anything. Females were allowed no share in the inheritance of their husbands, parents and other relatives. Men could marry as many women as they liked. Such was the condition of Arabia in pre-Islamic days *(Jahiliyyah)*.

Abdul Muttalib and Abdullah

During the fifth and sixth centuries, the ruling tribe of Makkah was the Quraish - direct descendants of Prophet Ibrahim. Qusayy, one of the leaders of the Quraish, became ruler over Makkah. It was in his house that the Quraish settled their affairs. Upon his death, his son Abdul Manaf, took over the leadership of the Quraish. Later, Hashim who was born in 464 AD, became Chief. It was Hashim who began the first two caravan journeys of the Quraish, one in summer to Syria and the north and one in the winter to Yemen and the South. As a result, Makkah grew rich and became an important trading centre. During the Pilgrimage season, Hashim entertained the pilgrims, providing them with bread and meat, butter, barley and dates.

Later in life, Hashim married Salma bint Amr Ibn Zaid who was from the tribe of Al Khasraj, a much respected family in Yathrib, and gave birth to a son named 'Shaybah'. However, Hashim died during a journey when Shaybah was just a child. Al Muttalib, Hashim's brother, took over the leadership. He brought Shaybah back to Makkah and upon entering the city the people of Makkah thought the boy was a slave and thus pointing at him, called out "Abd Al Muttalib!" Abd meaning slave. Al Muttalib explained that Shaybah was his nephew, nevertheless the people continued to call him Abd Al Muttalib.

During his leadership, Abdul Muttalib had to face opposition and struggled to retain his position. As it was his duty to provide water for the pilgrims; one of the major obstacles he encountered was the swelling up of the well of Zam-Zam. However, once in a dream, he was inspired to search between two of the idols placed near the Ka'bah. There he dug and the well of Zam-Zam was found.

In the course of time, Abdul Muttalib's situation improved and his wealth increased. He had acquired power and influence, but amidst all this prosperity, he had one source of sadness; he had only one son. He wanted many sons to succeed him and uphold the dignity of the family. Thus he vowed that if he ever were to have ten sons he would offer one of them in sacrifice.

Years passed by, several sons and daughters were born to him and eventually he had eleven sons. For a long time, Abdul Muttalib delayed the sacrifice, then the day arrived when he decided to fulfill his vow. Which of his sons was he to sacrifice? All were dear to him, especially the youngest son Abdullah. He decided to draw lots amongst them. The name of Abdullah came out and Abdul Muttalib was ready to fulfill his vow. However the people of Quraish protested. In this dilemma he was counselled by some wise men to visit a renowned soothsayer in Taif. She advised him to draw between the name 'Abdullah' and ten camels. If the name of Abdullah came out, he was to increase the number of camels each time by ten until the gods were appeased. So the lots were drawn in Makkah between ten camels and the life of Abdullah, but again the lots fell to him. Ten times in succession did the name of Abdullah appear and each time Abdul Muttalib increased the number of camels by ten; totalling one hundred camels. On the eleventh lot, the lots fell to the camel. A hundred camels were slaughtered and distributed amongst the poor.

When Abdullah reached the age of twenty four his father decided to marry him to Aminah, daughter of Wahb Ibn Manaf of the Zuhrah family. Some time after his marriage, Abdullah set out on a commercial journey to Syria and on his way back he fell ill and passed away in Yathrib at his maternal uncle's house. He was hardly twenty five years of age and Aminah was expectant with their child.

The Year of the Elephant

The year 571 AD was an important one in the history of Makkah. In that year the Chief of Yemen erected a church in his capital,

Sana, with a view to making it a commercial and religious centre in place of the Ka'bah, which he intended to demolish. He sent a large army which consisted of thirteen elephants to advance upon Makkah from the South and demolish the Ka'bah. Abraha Al Ashram rode at the head of the troops on a huge elephant named Mahmud.

In the meantime, Abdul Muttalib was grieving over the loss of his son, however, if Abraha succeeded in his aim it would be a greater loss. Hearing the news that some of his camels had been captured by Abraha, Abdul Muttalib went personally to him and demanded the camels back. Astonished by his response, Abraha said: "You are more worried about the camels than the Ka'bah, which I have come all this way to pull down." Abdul Muttalib replied: "Yes, I worry about my camels because I am their master, as to the Ka'bah; its Master will Himself look after it."

The Quraish tried to negotiate with Abraha, but to no avail. Abraha was determined to demolish the Ka'bah even after being offered one third of the wealth of the Thima region. He decided to attack the Ka'bah in the morning. He put on his armour and organised his troops. However, his elephants refused to move and would kneel down when faced towards Makkah. At the same time flocks of birds appeared from over the seas; each bird carrying stones slightly bigger than lentil seeds. When the stones were dropped over Abraha's army, the soldiers died with pain and Abraha died on his way back to Yemen.

After this incident, the Quraish gained respect and became known as 'the people of Allah'.

The Qur'an says :

أَلَمْ تَرَ كَيْفَ فَعَلَ رَبُّكَ بِأَصْحَٰبِ ٱلْفِيلِ ۝ أَلَمْ يَجْعَلْ كَيْدَهُمْ
فِى تَضْلِيلٍ ۝ وَأَرْسَلَ عَلَيْهِمْ طَيْرًا أَبَابِيلَ ۝ تَرْمِيهِم
بِحِجَارَةٍ مِّن سِجِّيلٍ ۝ فَجَعَلَهُمْ كَعَصْفٍ مَّأْكُولٍ ۝

Have you not seen how your Lord dealt with the owners of the elephant? Did
He not make their plot go astray? And send against them birds, in flocks
Striking them with stones of Sijjil. And made them like an empty field of stalks.

(Al Fil 105 : v 1-5)

BIRTH OF MUHAMMAD

In the same year, on Monday 12th Rabiul Awwal, in the early hours of the morning, a child was born to Aminah. This was the son of Abdullah, destined to be the Prophet of Revolution, bringing Arabia under the total submission and worship of One Allah.

When the news of the birth of a grandson was brought to Abdul Muttalib, he went to the house of Aminah and taking the child in his arms carried him to the Ka'bah to thank God. He named the child 'Muhammad', meaning 'the Praised One'. The leaders of the Quraish, upon hearing the name, asked why such a unique name was given. Abdul Muttalib replied: "I want him to be praised by Allah in the heavens and praised by men on earth."

Infancy

Shortly after his birth he was given to Thuwaybah, the slave girl of Abu Lahab who was one of the uncles of the Prophet. Though nursed by her only for a few days the Prophet retained a deep sense of kinship and treated her with respect and gratitude later in life.

It was the general custom amongst the wealthy Arab nobles to give their children into the care of bedouin nurses, so that they may grow up in the free and healthy surroundings of the desert, whereby they would develop the manners of bedouins. The bedouins were noted for the chastity of their language and for being free from those evils which were widespread in Makkah.

For a few days Muhammad was nursed by Aminah then he was entrusted to Halimah, a bedouin woman from the tribe of Banu Sa'd. Initially she was reluctant to nurse him, since the reward was likely to be less with an orphan child. However, all the other women of Banu Sa'd had found a child to take back with them; she did not want to be the only woman to go back to her tribe without a baby to bring up. On the return journey, as soon as Halimah began to feed Muhammad, her milk suddenly increased and she had enough for him as well as for her baby son.

During Muhammad's stay under the care of Halimah, her household was favoured by successive strokes of good fortune. The land became fertile, the date trees produced excess amount of dates, even the sheep and the old she-camel began to give milk.

Two years later, Halimah brought the child back to Aminah. At that time, Makkah was stricken by an epidemic, thus Aminah allowed Halimah to take Muhammad back with her.

It was also during the stay with Halimah, that two men who were in reality angels, came and cleansed Muhammad's heart. The foster brother of Muhammad had witnessed this incident and later told his mother who was naturally concerned. Allah had purified the heart of Muhammad for He intended him to be greater than any other human being ever born and the seal of the Prophets. The Qur'an says:

أَلَمْ نَشْرَحْ لَكَ صَدْرَكَ ۝ وَوَضَعْنَا عَنكَ وِزْرَكَ ۝ ٱلَّذِىٓ
أَنقَضَ ظَهْرَكَ ۝ وَرَفَعْنَا لَكَ ذِكْرَكَ ۝ فَإِنَّ مَعَ ٱلْعُسْرِ يُسْرًا ۝ إِنَّ
مَعَ ٱلْعُسْرِ يُسْرًا ۝ فَإِذَا فَرَغْتَ فَٱنصَبْ ۝ وَإِلَىٰ رَبِّكَ فَٱرْغَب ۝

41

Have We not opened your breast for you? And removed from you your
burden which weighed down your back? And raised high your fame.
So verily, with hardship there is relief. Verily with hardship there is relief. So
when you have finished, stand up for Allah's worship
And to your Lord turn your invocations.
(Ash-Sharh 94 : v 1-8)

The child grew up to be strong, healthy and learnt pure, chaste
Arabic of the desert. Even during his childhood he developed the
habit of reflection and ponderence.

Childhood

Muhammad remained with Halimah for six years and returned to
Aminah. She decided to take him to Yathrib to visit some relatives
and pay a visit to the tomb of Abdullah. It was on the return
journey from Yathrib that she fell ill and died. She was buried at a
place called Al Abwa situated between Makkah and Yathrib.
Barakah, the slave girl of Aminah, brought Muhammad back to
Abdul Muttalib in Makkah, who was distressed by the news. It was
more devastating for Muhammad, who was only six years old, now
lost both his mother and father.

The responsibility of looking after Muhammad fell on Abdul
Muttalib. He took care of Muhammad as he would take care of his
own son. However, Muhammad was again to be faced with sad
news; two years later, at the age of eighty-two, Abdul Muttalib
died.

Life as a Shepherd

After the death of Abdul Muttalib, Muhammad went into the care of his uncle Abu Talib. All the fortune that he inherited from his father was a flock of goats, five camels and a slave girl. He could not read or write as education was almost unheard of in Arabia. Like all other young boys of his age, he tended the sheep and goats in Makkah at a place known as the Ajyad. This occupation of tending goats suited his solitary, thoughtful and meditative temperament. It formed the training ground for the guidance of mankind. The shepherd is always alert about the flocks, taking full care that they do not go astray and are saved from any possible dangers. This is also the case with Prophets. They are shepherds of humanity, always thinking about the betterment of people and warning them of the dangers. Thus almost all of the Prophets sent by Allah, spent some time as shepherds.

Expedition to Syria

At the age of twelve, Muhammad undertook a business trip to Syria with his uncle Abu Talib. Abu Talib being fond of his nephew accepted to take him along on such a long journey. It was on this trip that he met Bahirah, a Christian monk. Bahirah saw the caravan in which Muhammad and his uncle were travelling, and noticed a large white cloud shading one of the travellers. He knew from the scriptures that another Prophet was to come after Prophet Isa (Jesus) and wanted to find more about the travellers in the caravan.

The monk sent an invitation to the caravan to come and eat with him. Abu Talib and the others travelling with him were surprised; many times they had passed Bahirah and he had never invited them. After insisting that the boy Muhammad should join them, he began observing him. Many of the physical features matched the description found in the scriptures. After the meal, Bahirah took Muhammad aside and asked a question swearing by the idols al Lat and al Uzza. Muhammad replied: "Do not ask by al Lat and al Uzza, for by God there is absolutely nothing I detest as much as these two." After further questioning Bahirah was satisfied that this was the Prophet mentioned in the scriptures. He returned to Abu Talib and said: "Return to your country with your nephew, and take care of him against the Jews, for by God, if they see him and know what I know about him, they will desire evil; for great fortune is in store for your nephew. So hurry to your country with him." Abu Talib returned to Makkah, heeding Bahirah's advice.

LIFE AS A YOUTH

Muhammad, ever since he was a boy, did not associate himself with playful children or waste time in idleness. Despite the prevailing environment of corruption, gambling, drinking and other social evils, he kept himself aloof. He never bowed before the idols and always refused to take meat which was sacrificed for idols and brought to him. He had the protection of Allah from committing evil deeds. As on one occasion, he went with some boys to a wedding in Makkah. When he reached the house, he heard sounds of music and dancing and suddenly felt tired and fell asleep. He awoke the following morning, thus missing the celebrations.

Battle of Fujjar and Hilful Fudhul

A war broke out in Makkah during the Hajj season between the tribes of Quraish and Qays Aylan at Ukas. These wars continued for four years, even though according to Makkan traditions, war was forbidden during the Hajj season. Muhammad was fifteen years of age and participated in one of those wars known as Harb al Fujjar. He never raised arms against his opponents as his efforts were confined to picking up the arrows of the enemy as they fell and handing them over to his uncle.

At the conclusion of these wars, the Makkans decided that a body was required to suppress violence and injustice and help the weak and needy. Az Zubair, one of Muhammad's uncles, invited him to the meeting at the house of Abdullah ibn Sudan. At this meeting a society called 'Hilful Fudhul' was formed; Muhammad played an important part in its formation. Later during the days of his

Prophethood, he once recalled this incident and said: "In return for this pledge I will not accept a gift of red camels and even now if I am called upon for such a pledge, I will not refuse."

Trading Expeditions

Muhammad led a quiet life with his uncle Abu Talib in Makkah. At the age of twenty five, he chose the profession of trade, in which the most prominent capitalists wished to invest their money through him, because traders like Sai'b, Qais Ibn Saib Makzumi and Khadijah had already had practical experience of his character, integrity and fair dealings. It was for his honest and honorouble character that they gave him the title 'Al Ameen' the Trustworthy.

Abdullah Ibn Abil Hamsa, once asked Muhammad to stay at a place and wait for him; but Hamsa forgot about it. After three full days when he passed by that way, he found Muhammad there waiting for him.

Muhammad was later entrusted with the merchandise of Khadijah, daughter of Khuwaylid. During the negotiations Khadijah told Abu Talib: "I would give him double, what I would give to other men of your tribe." The first journey Muhammad made was to Syria. He was accompanied by Maysarah the servant of Khadijah.

Two unusual incidents occurred during this journey. The caravan had taken the usual route to Syria. On the road to Damascus Muhammad sat down to rest under a shady tree.

A Christian monk upon seeing this rushed up to the spot and asked

46

Maysarah the identity of the person sitting under the tree. He was told by Maysarah that it was someone from the Quraish. "Right from Jesus, son of Mary, no one ever sat there but a Prophet. He is the Prophet and the last of the Apostles," said the monk.

Muhammad proceeded towards Syria and conducted the sale of the merchandise, making a profit, larger than usual. On the way back to Makkah, the second unusual event occurred and was again noticed by Maysarah. It happened at noon when the sun was at its hottest. Maysarah was riding behind Muhammad and noticed that he was protected from the heat of the sun by clouds, as had occurred in the previous journey to Syria.

Marriage to Khadijah

On returning to Makkah, Maysarah related everything that had occurred to Khadijah. Khadijah being immensely impressed with the character of Muhammad decided to marry him. Hafisa, a friend of Khadijah was sent to Muhammad to enquire as to why he had not married. "I have nothing in my hands with which I can meet the expenses of the wedding," replied Muhammad. "What if that difficulty is removed and you are invited to marry a beautiful wealthy lady of a noble birth?" asked Hafisa. Upon hearing it was Khadijah, he agreed. Khadijah's noble character was well known amongst the people of Makkah and many men had proposed to her since the death of her husband, but she had refused them all and was now prepared to marry Muhammad.

On the appointed day, Muhammad along with his uncle Abu Talib and Hamza and several other chiefs of his tribe went to Khadijah's house. It was her uncle Amr Ibn Al Aas who gave her hand in marriage to him. Khadijah was forty years old and Muhammad twenty five at the time of the marriage. Abu Talib performed the marriage service in the following words:

"There is no-one to compare with my nephew Muhammad Ibn Abdullah. He outshines everyone in nobility, gentility; eminence and wisdom. By God, he has a great future and will reach a very high station."

Abu Talib did not utter these words in the sense in which later events proved them to be true; rather he meant them in a worldly sense. Muhammad paid Khadijah a dowry of twenty bakras according to the customs of the Arabs.

From the time of the marriage, for quarter of a century, Khadijah gave him ease of circumstances, freedom from the cares of daily life, strength and comfort of deep mutual love.

Ka'bah and its Re-building

Muhammad lived a calm and quiet life as a merchant in Makkah. He had no materialistic desire as was the prevailing case amongst the capitalist merchants. More than anything, his wisdom benefited the people of Makkah and prevented bloodshed. On one occasion the Quraish decided to rebuild the Ka'bah, as it was threatened with destruction by another flood. The fear of tampering with such a building provided an obstacle; all were in awe and fear. Eventually, Al Walid Ibn Al Mughirah, called upon the gods of the Ka'bah, then took a pick-axe and pulled down a part of the wall. People waited, realising that nothing would happen, they all joined in the re-building of the Ka'bah. When the walls were at an appropriate height they decided to place the black stone on the east wall of the Ka'bah. A dispute arose amongst the people as to which tribe will have the honour of placing the stone in its correct place. Arguments continued for four days and daggers were nearly on a point of being drawn. On the fifth day Umayyah Ibn Mughirah, the oldest amongst the chiefs, made a proposal which was accepted by all. He suggested that the first person to enter the courtyard of the Ka'bah on the following day by the eastern gate, should be accepted as judge and asked to decide the matter.

The next morning, Muhammad was the first to enter the courtyard. The people from all of the tribes cried in one voice: "Al Ameen has come, we agree to abide by his decision." The situation was explained to him and he at once resolved the dispute. He spread his cloak on the ground and placed the black stone upon it with his own hands. He then asked representatives from each tribe to lift the cloak among them together. When the black stone had been raised to the required height from the ground, Muhammad himself set it in its place in the south east corner of the Ka'bah.

Craving for the Truth

Muhammad would reflect and contemplate about society and the human race. His heart was filled with sadness at the situation. He would seclude himself from society and find momentary places of solitary confinement. The Cave Hira in Mount Nur was one of his favourite resorts. His heart continuously sought to comprehend the mysteries of creation, life and death, good and evil. He knew that there had to be One Creator and All Mighty.

He had all conceivable means and opportunities for a comfortable life, but his troubled soul did not find satisfaction in them. He attached no value to them and could not rest until he solved the answers to the mysteries of life. Where did humans come from? What is the purpose of their creation? What will happen to them after they die? The most important question of all was the question Truth *(Haq)* and Falsehood *(Batil)*. This phase of his life is referred to in the Qur'an:

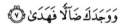

And He found you unaware and guided you?
(Ad-Duha 93 : v 7)

Not only was Muhammad craving for the Truth; some sensible people within the Makkan society were also awaiting divine guidance and were disgusted with the darkness prevailing in their society. On one occasion, whilst the Quraish were celebrating a festival, singing praises of their idols; Waraqa Ibn Nawfal, Abdullah Ibn Jahsh, Uthman Ibn Al Thuwayris and Zaid Ibn Amr were holding a secret meeting and taking pledges of secrecy. They agreed that their community had deviated and had drifted from the religion of Prophet Ibrahim and were in a state of delusion: worshipping idols made out of stone. All four resolved to go about in the search of the followers of Ibrahim.

Waraqa Ibn Nawfal became a Christian. Abdullah Ibn Jahsh in his restlessness first adopted Islam (after the Prophethood of Muhammad) and later became a Christian. Uthman went to the

Emperor of Rome and also became a Christian. However Zaid did not adopt any other religion and continued the search for truth; although he had given up idol worshipping, refrained from eating the food sacrificed for the idols and preached against the killing of the new born daughters. He would often say: "God should be one or a thousand. Is it that a religion that divides its affairs among so many deities?" Many times when he used to enter the Ka'bah he would say: "I am present my Lord, as an obedient worshipping servant with all sincerity."

He also used to pray that he was seeking the protection of the Lord whose protection was sought by Prophet Ibrahim. Khattab Ibn Nufayl hated Zaid for these actions and thus drove him out of Makkah, sending some young boys to make sure that he did not try to return back to Makkah. Wherever Zaid went secretly he was driven out and beaten by those boys. Finally in despair he left the country and wandered about in Iraq and Syria. In Damascus he met a monk who told him that he will not find any followers of Prophet Ibrahim anywhere; however a Prophet would be raised from Makkah and will proclaim the way of Ibrahim. Upon hearing this, Zaid travelled back towards Makkah but someone killed him at a place known as Lakhim.

Qur'an is Revealed

It was the month of Ramadhan in the year 609 AD. Muhammad was forty but still retreating to Cave Hira. It was on one of these nights that Allah communicated with him through Angel Jibrail. Whilst he was sleeping, the angel suddenly appeared and commanded him to "Read!" "I cannot read," Muhammad replied.

51

The angel then squeezed him vehemently and then let him go, again repeating the order "Read!" Muhammad again gave the same reply: "I cannot read." The angel again squeezed him, this process was repeated three times until the angel said:

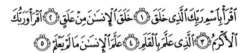

Read in the name of your Lord, Who has created (all that exists),
Has created man from a clot.
Read ! And your Lord is the Most Generous.
Who has taught by the pen. Has taught man that which he knew not.
(Iqrah 96 : v 1-5)

These were the first five verses revealed to Muhammad. The words had been inscribed on his heart and branded on his soul. At first he could not comprehend what was happening and he was slightly scared. He went out of the cave and started coming down the mountain when he heard the voice again, this time saying: "O Muhammad! You are the Messenger of Allah and I am Angel Jibrail." Prophet Muhammad turned his face around and saw Angel Jibrail. He tried to turn his face away from the brightness of the vision, but whichever direction he turned his face, there stood Angel Jibrail facing him.

Khadijah and Waraqa Ibn Nawfal

Prophet Muhammad returned home to Khadijah after the incident. Upon seeing him shivering, as though he had a fever, she wrapped him in a blanket and told him to rest. He recovered enough to tell her what had happened in Cave Hira. Khadijah believed all that he told her and comforted him saying: "Truly, I swear by Allah who has my soul in His Hands that you will be the nation's Prophet. Allah will surely not desert you, for you are kind to your family, you help the helpless, you make guests welcome, you support the weak and the oppressed."

Khadijah began to ponder over the events and later decided to relate everything to Waraqa Ibn Nawfal, her Christian cousin. Waraqa at once replied: "This is the very Angel that God sent down to Musa. It seems that God has chosen Muhammad for His work. He is the Prophet of the nation. His people will try to drive him out and he will be persecuted. If I am alive then, God knows that I will help His Cause."

From that day, the beginning of the revelation of the Qur'an began. A short time after the first revelation Angel Jibrail appeared in a vision revealing:

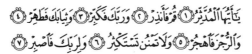

O you enveloped in garments.
Arise and warn. And your Lord magnify.
And your garments purify.
And keep away from the idols.
And give not a thing in order to have more.
And be patient for the sake of your Lord.
(Al Mudaththir 74 : v 1-7)

THE MISSION AND THE MOVEMENT

The analysis of the above ayahs (verses), provided the Prophet Muhammad three stages for the cause in which he was to strive for:

1. Personal reform, so that one worships Allah alone in totality and avoids all forms of wrong doings and disobedience *(Al Islahul Fardi)*.

2. Impressing on others the reality of their existence and final destiny; that they are Allah's servants and will return to Him after death *(Da'wah and Inzaar)*; hence establishing the rule of Islam in society *(Iqamat ud Deen)*.

3. Remaining steadfast in the face of difficulties and opposition which afflicts oneself when attempting to reform both oneself and society *(As Sabr wal Istiqamah)*.

The verses proved to be a turning point in the life of Prophet Muhammad. He would no longer retreat into continual solitary confinement; rather he was now entrusted with the duty of conveying the message of Islam to mankind *(Da'wah)* and initiating a movement for the dominance of Islam over all other ways of life *(Al Harakatul Islamiyyah)*. He was not to change society partially; as it is futile to implement partial good in some aspects of life. Partial good can be seen in every mission and even in bad systems there is a random good.

Thus the message of Islam was not to be a negative protest against the existing order but a comprehensive ideal and a system of life

(Nizam un Shamil) for a collective transformation of society. The mission was total reform of life; social upliftment, the establishment of the rule of Allah in order to be His slave.

The Prophet realised from the outset that his mission would be difficult to accomplish. For a period, revelation ceased and the Prophet began to worry, thinking that Allah had forsaken him. However Angel Jibrail came with the following verses:

وَٱلضُّحَىٰ ۝ وَٱلَّيْلِ إِذَا سَجَىٰ ۝ مَا وَدَّعَكَ رَبُّكَ وَمَا قَلَىٰ ۝
وَلَلْآخِرَةُ خَيْرٌ لَّكَ مِنَ ٱلْأُولَىٰ ۝ وَلَسَوْفَ يُعْطِيكَ رَبُّكَ
فَتَرْضَىٰ ۝ أَلَمْ يَجِدْكَ يَتِيمًا فَـَٔاوَىٰ ۝ وَوَجَدَكَ ضَآلًّا
فَهَدَىٰ ۝ وَوَجَدَكَ عَآئِلًا فَأَغْنَىٰ ۝ فَأَمَّا ٱلْيَتِيمَ فَلَا تَقْهَرْ
۝ وَأَمَّا ٱلسَّآئِلَ فَلَا تَنْهَرْ ۝ وَأَمَّا بِنِعْمَةِ رَبِّكَ فَحَدِّثْ ۝

By the forenoon; And by the night when it is still; Your Lord has neither forsaken you nor hated you. And indeed the hereafter is better for you than the present. And verily your Lord will give you so that you may be pleased. Did He not find you an orphan and gave you a refuge. And He found you unaware and guided you. And He found you poor and made you rich. Therefore, treat not the orphan with oppression and repulse not the beggar.
And proclaim the grace of your Lord.
(Ad-Duha 93 : v 1-11)

Stage of Secret Da'wah

Khadijah was the first person as well as the first woman to embrace the message of Islam: to declare that there is no God but Allah and Muhammad is His slave and Messenger. The Prophet then began the Da'wah secretly *(Ad Da'wah as Sirriyyah)* to those who were close to him.

It was also during this period, when the Prophet was outside the city of Makkah, that Jibrail appeared to him. Jibrail kicked the side of a hill and a spring of water began to flow out. He then began to wash himself with the water to show the Prophet the ritual ablution (*wudu*) to be made before the prayers.

Ali Ibn Abu Talib Enters Islam

During this time, Makkah was facing economic difficulties. There was a shortage of food. Abu Talib, the Prophet's uncle was finding it difficult to feed his large family. The Prophet offered to take care of Ali, the son of Abu Talib, whilst Abbas, another uncle of the Prophet, took care of Jafar Ibn Abu Talib.

Once Ali came into the Prophet's house and saw the Prophet and Khadijah praying in a strange manner. He asked the Prophet as to what they were doing. The Prophet then explained the message of Islam to him. Ali responded by saying: "I have heard nothing of this nature before and cannot make a decision until I have talked the matter over with my father." But the Prophet did not want anyone to know of the message of Islam until the time had come for it to be made public. "Ali" he said, "If you are not ready to become a Muslim; then keep the matter to yourself."

Ali waited for one night and Allah guided his heart towards Islam. He went back to the Prophet early in the morning. "What was it that you were telling me yesterday?" he asked. The Prophet replied: "Bear witness that there is none worthy of worship except Allah. He is One and has no partner. Forsake the idols al Lat and al Uzza and disown all those who are set up as equals with Allah." Ali accepted this and became a Muslim. Then in fear of Abu Talib he used to come to see the Prophet secretly. However, once while the Prophet, Khadijah and Ali were praying, Abu Talib happened to pass by and when he saw them, he asked what they were doing. The Prophet explained that like Prophet Ibrahim he was praying and was told to guide people to the Truth. Abu Talib looked at his son Ali and said: "Muhammad would never make you do anything that was wrong. Go with him but I cannot leave the religion which I follow and which was followed by my father." Then he turned to the Prophet and said: "Even so, I promise you Muhammad that no-one will hurt you whilst I am alive. You have my full protection." This support proved to be crucial in later years to come.

Ali was only ten years old when he accepted Islam and was joined shortly after Zaid Ibn Harith, a freed slave adopted by the Prophet. Again Zaid was only a young boy when he accepted Islam.

Abu Bakr Enters Islam

The first man to accept Islam was Abu Bakr the closest friend of the Prophet and a well known figure of the Quraish. When the message of Islam was presented before him, he responded by saying: "I swear by my father and mother that you have never told a lie and I know that you would not say anything about God that is not true. I know, therefore that there is only One God and that you are the Messenger of God."

Regarding the acceptance of Islam by Abu Bakr, the Prophet later said: "I have never invited anyone to the faith, who did not display some hesitation in embracing it, except Abu Bakr. As for Abu Bakr, when I offered Islam, he showed no hesitation, not even the least."

From the day Abu Bakr embraced Islam, he dedicated all his time and energy to the propagation of the Divine faith of Islam. Very few could equal him in his determination and sacrifice.

Khadijah, Abu Bakr, Ali and Zaid were the closest people to the Prophet. They knew the character and truthfulness of the Prophet better than others. They did not have a shadow of doubt that Muhammad was the Prophet of Allah. The fact that those nearest to him and fully acquainted with every detail of his life and character, were the first to enter into the faith, proves its absolute truth.

The First Muslims

Abu Bakr was instrumental in the Da'wah of Islam during the secret stage. The earliest converts to Islam were those who had been closely associated with him. Sa'd Ibn Abi Waqqas, Zubayr Ibn Al Awwam, Uthman Ibn Affan, Abdur Rahman Ibn Awf and Talha Ibn Ubaydullah were the first Muslims. Zubayr was only fourteen when he embraced Islam.

Abu Bakr once went into the house of Umayyah Ibn Khalaf; a prominent man amongst the Quraish. Upon learning that he was not at home, he decided to talk to Umayyah's slave, Bilal, about Islam and subsequently Bilal became a Muslim.

The determined workers of Islam began to spread the message secretly and in due course Arqam Ibn Abi Arqam, Ubaydullah Ibn

Harith, Saeed Ibn Zayd, Amr Ibn Nufayl and his wife, Fatimah wife of Saeed Ibn Zayd, Asma the daughter of Abu Bakr, Abdullah Ibn Masud, Jafar Ibn Abu Talib, Uthman Ibn Maznoon and Suhaib Al Rumi made up the group of believers during the secret phase of Da'wah.

Among those who had become Muslims, there was a group who had been believers in the unity of Allah, even though it was not in total agreement with the Islamic belief *(Al Aqeedatul Islamiyyah)*, seeds of righteousness existed within their hearts. Saeed Ibn Zayd was one of the most notable amongst this group. There were others who stood outside the clan system. They were in no way inferior to the Quraish but they did not have a clan to support them and did not have power nor influence in the Makkan society. Amongst them were Ammar, Kabbab and Abu Fukayka Shuayb.

When the Prophet had gathered thirty eight believers around him, Abu Bakr urged to publicise the mission. He was of the opinion that they should go out into the open and publicly preach the message of Islam. But the Prophet said to him: "No Abu Bakr, we are too few." Thus for three years the message of Islam was spread in a secret and organised manner.

During this stage, opposition was very minimal as the Da'wah was not done in public. The leaders of the Quraish did not care much for Prophet Muhammad and his teachings and thought that it was the act of some unbalanced young man who would soon repent to the Quraish. It was thought that no movement would succeed in Makkah in the presence of the idols. Prophet Muhammad and the companions were merely scoffed and laughed at.

Stage of Open Da'wah

Upon the completion of the third year, Allah revealed the following verses:

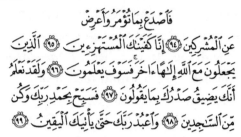

Therefore proclaim openly that which you are commanded,
and turn away from the polytheists.
Truly We will suffice you against the scoffers who set up
along with Allah another god, they will come to know.
Indeed We know that your breast is straitened at what
they say. So glorify the praises of your Lord
and be of those who prostrate themselves.

(Al Hijr 15 : v 94-98)

Allah had now told the Prophet to proclaim the message of Islam in public *(Ad Da'wah Al-A'laniyyah)*. The Prophet went on top of Mount Safa, as was the usual custom for calling people. The usual custom was to ascend the mountain naked, as to attract attention. However the Prophet ascended Mount Safa wearing his clothes and thus a pre-Islamic method was used within the limits of Islam.

People gathered to hear what he had to say. The Prophet called out: "O People of Quraish! Were I to tell you that an army was advancing to attack you from behind this mountain, will you believe me?" "Yes, why not? We have always found you to be truthful." Looking at each sub-division of the Quraish clan the Prophet continued: "O Banu Abdul Muttalib! O Banu Abd Manaf! O Banu Zuhrah! I have come to you as a Warner and if you do not respond to my warning, punishment will fall upon you. I have been commanded by God to warn you and I cannot protect you in this world, nor can I promise you anything in the next world, unless you acknowledge and submit to the worship of One Allah." At this stage Abu Lahab, one of the uncles of the Prophet and an elite amongst the Quraish, interrupted and said: "May you perish, did you call us for this ?" The crowd then dispersed.

Regarding the insult by Abu Lahab, Allah revealed the following verses to console the Prophet:

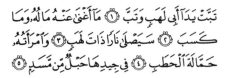

Perish the hands of Abu Lahab and perish he.
His wealth and his children will not benefit him.
He will be burnt in a fire of blazing flames.
And his wife, the carrier of fire wood.
Shall have a rope of palm-fibre around her neck.
(Al Masad 111 : v 1-5)

Regardless of what had happened, the Prophet had invited the family of Abdul Muttalib to a dinner, after which he intended to deliver a message. Again Abu Lahab interrupted and made a mockery and the people dispersed. He invited the family again for a second dinner and this time explained what was at stake. He said: "I know of no man in the land of Arabia who can place before his people a more excellent offer than which I now make to you. I offer you the happiness of this world and that of the next. So who will help me in my cause?" Everybody kept silent until a child came forward and said: "I have sore eyes, my legs are weak and I am yet still a child, yet I will follow you and help you in this mission. I will be at war against those who fight you." That child was Ali Ibn Abu Talib. Others present began to laugh amongst themselves, joking as to what change Prophet Muhammad could bring with a follower like Ali.

Prophet Muhammad's enthusiasm in his efforts to communicate the faith to others is incomparable. He would seek every opportunity to convey the message of Islam. Once the leaders of the Quraish had gathered around the Ka'bah and called for the Prophet. He came quickly thinking that they might be inclining towards Islam; the fact that they would be thrown into the fires of Hell *(Jahannam)* disturbed him. However, it happened that they wanted to pick a quarrel and the acceptance of Islam was the last thing on their minds. The Prophet returned home sad and disillusioned, for the hopes he had for his people when they called him, had been dashed. He had seen how far people were from accepting the message of Islam.

Day and night he was busy in preaching the word of Allah. His Da'wah was far from an obvious repetition of certain set speeches. He used to take into consideration the nature of his audience before formulating his message *(Hikmat ud Da'wah)*:

On one occasion the Prophet invited Abu Sufyan and his wife to Islam with the following words: "O Abu Sufyan Ibn Harb! O Hind bint Utbah! You are going to die and then you will be raised up. The good will be admitted into Heaven *(Jannah)* and the bad will enter Hell; I am telling you the Truth."

When inviting Haseen, he asked him: "Tell me Haseen, how many gods do you worship?" "Seven on earth and one in heaven," replied Haseen. "Whom do you call on when you are in trouble?" the Prophet asked. "The one in heaven," answered Haseen. "And whom do you call on when you have suffered loss of wealth?" the Prophet asked again. "The one in heaven," came the same reply. "He alone answers your prayers" the Prophet said, "Then why do you set up others as His equals?"

Abu Umamah once came to the Prophet and asked him what teachings he had brought from Allah. The Prophet's reply was that relationships should be strengthened and wrongful killings avoided. Roads should be left open and the idols should be broken. Only One God should be worshipped and no others set up with him as His equals.

The Prophet even promised the people power if they accepted Islam: "It is only one phrase; and if you accept that from me, the whole of Arabia will be under your rule and also the non-Arab lands." At other times, he used to address the leaders of tribes saying: "Take me with you and let me have the chance to work and co-operate with you till I have explained the mission for which Allah has sent me."

Bahira Ibn Firas, chief of Banu Amir was impressed by the Prophet's personality, mission and devoted zeal that he declared: "If we accept this young man and include him amongst us, we will dominate the whole of Arabia." He saw a bright future for Islam and tried to negotiate a bargain with the Prophet. He offered to co-operate with the Prophet on the condition that when all opposition had been subdued, the Prophet would transfer power to him. The Prophet replied: "Power is in the hands of Allah and He confers it to whomsoever He likes," and refused to accept Bahira's proposal.

Reaction to the Da'wah

The initial reaction of the masses of Makkah was negative. Some were only familiar with religion in a particular conventional form. To them, the message of Islam, appeared to be an insult to their ancestors. Dhamad once came to Makkah and sat down with Abu Jahl, Utbah Ibn Rabiah and Umayyah Ibn Khalfa. Abu Jahl, referring to the Prophet, said to them: "He has caused a split in our community and thinks we are fools and insults our idols. He considers our ancestors to be on the wrong path." Umayyah added: "Without a doubt he is insane."

The jealousy of some people prevented them from accepting Islam. Some found it difficult to accept that someone other than themselves had been given the knowledge of reality. Abu Jahl once took the Prophet aside and said to him: "By God, I know full well that what you say is the Truth, but one thing stops me from believing. The tribe of Banu Qussay say that they are the gate keepers of the Ka'bah; I agree. They say it is their responsibility to carry the flag in battles; I agree with that. They say it is their duty to provide water for the pilgrims; I agree with that. Now they say that you are a Prophet amongst them, I cannot accept this."

The elite of the Makkan society did not want to accept Islam as it would affect them politically; in terms of power, and economically; in terms of their exploitation. They realised that worshipping idols, killing girls, drinking, gambling, cheating and oppressing the poor would be outlawed if Islam was established in the society. The Ka'bah was one of their main sources of economic exploitation; were the idols to be removed they would lose a great deal of money. Material wealth and status were two evils to which they attached great importance.

However, the most common reaction amongst the masses was based on ignorance. When Amr Ibn Murr was giving Da'wah amongst his people, one of them spoke up: "May God make you taste the bitterness of life. Amr, do you want us to forsake our idols, disunite our people and contradict the religion of our forefathers. He who seeks to prove that our forefathers were fools, cannot prosper."

RIDICULE AND PROPAGANDA

During the three years of the secret phase of Da'wah, opposition was hardly seen. However, when the Quraish realised that Prophet Muhammad was gaining followers and support day by day, they felt threatened and decided to combat the spread of Islam.

The opposition itself had stages. It started with ridicule and joking. The Quraish used to point towards people like Ali, Ammar and Khabbab and ask the Prophet with scorn and jest: "Are these the only people who have been blessed by Allah amongst us?" They would also ridicule and hurl abuse whilst the Prophet and his companions were praying in the mountain pass.

However, ridiculing did not stop the growth of the Prophet's movement for Islam. The Quraish thus started a propaganda campaign. People were prevented from listening to him by alleging that he was not religious. He was nicknamed 'Abu Kabsha', the father of Kabsha (who was a worshipper of stars, against the general custom of the Arabs). They told people that he had become mentally unbalanced due to the curses of the idols. He was called a poet and a soothsayer due to the content and extraordinary literary excellence of the revelations. The Qur'an answers their propaganda:

It is not the word of a poet, little is that you believe.
Nor is it the word of a soothsayer, little is that you
remember.

(Al Haqqah 69 : v 41-42)

66

It was also alleged that the revelation of the Qur'an was not the word of Allah, but forged by the Prophet. Again the Qur'an refutes this allegation by challenging the Quraish:

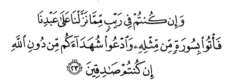

And if you are in doubt concerning that which We have
sent down to Our slave; then produce a surah of the
like thereof and call your witnesses besides Allah
if you are truthful.

(Al Baqarah 2 : v 23)

They further alleged that if the Qur'an was really from God, why not let the Qur'an itself descend from the heaven or the Prophet himself ascend to the heaven and bring the book.

The Quraish tried their utmost to ensure that people did not listen to the revelation because it had a profound effect on the listener of whom some became Muslims. The Qur'an refers to this propaganda:

وَقَالَ ٱلَّذِينَ كَفَرُوا۟ لَا تَسْمَعُوا۟ لِهَٰذَا ٱلْقُرْءَانِ وَٱلْغَوْا۟ فِيهِ لَعَلَّكُمْ تَغْلِبُونَ ۝

"And those who disbelieve say: Listen not to this Qur'an and make noise in the
midst of its (recitation) that you may overcome."

(Al Fussilat 41 : v 26)

Hazr Ibn Harith, a prominent figure of the Quraish, devised a plan to mock the Qur'an and deviate the people. He often used to travel to Persia for business dealings and from there bought stories of ancient heroes of Persia in addition to the fiction of the region. He would collect people around him to listen; insisting that the stories of Rustham and Asfhandiar were more interesting than the stories of Aad and Thamud in the Qur'an. About such people the Qur'an says:

$$وَمِنَ ٱلنَّاسِ مَن يَشۡتَرِى لَهۡوَ ٱلۡحَدِيثِ لِيُضِلَّ عَن سَبِيلِ ٱللَّهِ بِغَيۡرِ عِلۡمٍ وَيَتَّخِذَهَا هُزُوًاۚ أُوْلَـٰٓئِكَ لَهُمۡ عَذَابٌ مُّهِينٌ ٦$$

And of mankind is he who purchases idle talk to mislead from the path of Allah without knowledge and takes it by mockery for such there will be humiliating torment.

(Al Luqman 31 : v 6)

Opposition by ridicule and propaganda was unsuccessful and thus the Quraish resorted to violence on a small scale.

Attempts at Compromise

Violence against some of the Muslims was possible, but due to the support given by Abu Talib to Prophet Muhammad it was impossible to use violence against him. Such was the support that any attempt to abuse him would mean enmity with the whole clan of Banu Hashim. In order to avoid this the Quraish decided to persuade Abu Talib to withdraw his support. A deputation of influential people consisting of Utbah Ibn Rabiah, Abu Jahl, Al Walid Ibn Al Mughira, Nabia and Shabia sons of Rabia, Aas Ibn Walil and the sons of Hajar Ibn Amr was sent to Abu Talib.

They said to him: "O Abu Talib! Your nephew abuses and curses our gods, criticises and mocks our religion, degrades our forefathers and regards them on the wrong path; so you should either stop him or do not stand between us and your nephew." Abu Talib tried to calm them and sent them away with a polite reply. He then sent Aqeel, his son, to fetch Prophet Muhammad. When the Prophet arrived he related everything that happened and the Prophet responded by saying: "By Allah! Is anyone among you able to light a fire from a flame of the sun? Well, I am no more capable of that than I am of forsaking the mission Allah has entrusted me with." The Prophet continued his Da'wah activities, regardless of the dangers.

The Quraish were further infuriated and sent a second delegation to Abu Talib. It's leader said: "O Abu Talib! You hold an important position amongst us in respect of age and nobility. We had asked you to protect us from your nephew but you did not. The way he is criticising our idols is now beyond endurance. So unless you stop him from this we will fight both you and him till one of us is eliminated." Abu Talib was deeply distressed at the situation but he could not forsake his nephew. He sent for the Prophet and informed him of the second delegation saying: "Spare me and yourself and put not a burden upon me which I cannot bear."

The Prophet was faced with a great crisis: the only support which he could depend on was weakening. Nevertheless he replied in a voice that changed the course of history: "O My Uncle! By Allah if they were to put the sun in my right hand and the moon in my left hand on the condition that I abandon my mission; I will not do it until Allah has made me victorious or I lose my life in the struggle."

The Prophet got up and as he turned away, Abu Talib said: "Go and preach what you wish, for by God! I will never forsake you."

The Quraish decided to send a third delegation. The delegation this time brought Amara Ibn Walid, and its leader said to Abu Talib: "O Abu Talib! Do you see Amara Ibn Walid. He is a handsome strong young man. Take him and adopt him as your son. His wisdom and strength will serve you well and hand over Muhammad to us. He is continuously insulting our ancestors and disrupting our community. We will kill him and give Amara in his place." Abu Talib for a third time refused.

In view of the danger Abu Talib called together Banu Hashim and Banu Muttalib and appealed them to support the Prophet. The majority were willing to support the Prophet, but Abu Lahab strongly opposed them and the meeting ended without reaching a final decision.

In the meantime the message of Islam was spreading across Makkah and many of the Quraish were accepting the message. The Quraish decided to prevent people meeting the Prophet in order to limit the sphere of influence of the Da'wah.

On one such occasion, Tufayl Ibn Umar, a talented poet, came to Makkah. The Quraish immediately went to him and warned him: "O Tufayl! You have come to our city, but the activities of Muhammad are becoming intolerable for us. He has subverted our interests and disrupted our unity. His words are like magic. So we request you not to visit him nor talk to him, so as not to come under his spell." Tufayl was made to agree and every time he went to the Ka'bah he plugged his ears with cotton. Later he decided that, surely being a poet, he had the necessary knowledge to distinguish between good and evil; thus he would listen to the Prophet and if it was reasonable he would accept it, and if not, reject it. He met the Prophet and asked him to explain his message and mission. The Prophet did so, reciting verses from the Qur'an which touched the heart of Tufayl. He decided to become a Muslim and returning home propagated his new belief with such determination that his entire clan accepted Islam.

The Quraish realised the power of the words of Allah and wanted to compromise with the Prophet regarding it:

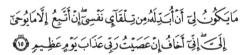

And when Our Clear Verses are recited unto them, those who hope not for
their meeting with Us, say: 'Bring us a Qur'an other than this or change it.'
(Yunus 10 : v 15)

The Prophet replied in the words of the revelation:

مَا يَكُونُ لِيٓ أَنْ أُبَدِّلَهُۥ مِن تِلْقَآئِ نَفْسِيٓۖ إِنْ أَتَّبِعُ إِلَّا مَا يُوحَىٰٓ
إِلَيَّۖ إِنِّيٓ أَخَافُ إِنْ عَصَيْتُ رَبِّي عَذَابَ يَوْمٍ عَظِيمٍ ۝

It is not for me to change it on my own accord;
I only follow that which is revealed unto me.
Verily I fear if I were to disobey my Lord,
the torment of the Great Day.
(Yunus 10 : v 15)

Persecution of the Believers

When the Quraish perceived that Abu Talib would continue to support for his nephew and that Prophet Muhammad would not forsake his mission, they decided to organise a campaign of persecution against the Muslims.

Bilal, the slave of Umayyah Ibn Khalaf, was severely beaten by his master when he came to know of his conversion to Islam. A rope was put around his neck and he was dragged through the streets of Makkah. At other times he was subjugated to prolonged deprivation of food and drink. He was thrown on the burning sand at noon time with a large stone placed on his back. When Umayyah said that he would die like this if he did not forsake Islam, Bilal's reply was: "One! One! One God!" Sometimes he was forced to put on a steel armour and seated in the hot sun. Abu Bakr was once passing by and purchased Bilal from Umayyah and freed him.

Khabbab Ibn Irth Tamimi was sold as a slave in the pre-Islamic days *(Jahiliyyah)* to Umm Numayr. He embraced Islam when the House of Arqam was the centre of the movement from where the Prophet used to organise *(Jama'ah)* and train the believers *(Tarbiyyah)*. When he was found to be a Muslim he was thrown on glowing cinders and a man was made to stand over him to make sure he did not turn sides. Later he showed his back to a companion who described it as 'all white' due to the persecution. His means of livelihood also stopped as people did not pay his dues.

Another victim of the campaign of persecution was Ammar Ibn Yasir. His entire family had accepted Islam and suffered cruel persecution. Since they were not original inhabitants of Makkah, they had no influential tribe to back them. Ammar was thrown on burning sand and severely beaten till he became unconscious. His father Yasir was thrown into water and forced to lie on glowing cinders. His mother Sumayyah was stabbed to death by Abu Jahl and became the first Muslim woman to be martyred. During their persecution, the Prophet would pass by and say to them: "Be patient, O family of Yasir! Jannah is your promised land."

Abu Fakih Juhani was another slave who was being tortured by his master Safwan Ibn Umayyah. He was dragged by his neck on the hot desert sand; and on the way Safwan saw a beetle and asked Abu Fakih: "Is that your God?" "My God is Allah and He is also your God," replied Abu Fakih. The answer enraged Safwan and he nearly strangled Abu Fakih to death. Fortunately Abu Fakih was later purchased and freed by Abu Bakr.

Lubayna and Zunayra, the slave girls of Umar Ibn Al Khattab (not yet a believer) were beaten severely by him. Zunayra lost her eyes after Abu Jahl mercilessly beat her. Abu Bakr also freed them.

Abdullah Ibn Masud on accepting Islam went to the Ka'bah to recite the Qur'an when Abu Jahl attacked him and beat him severely; yet he continued to recite. Uthman Ibn Affan was bound and beaten by his own uncle Al Hakm Ibn Al Aas. Khalid Ibn Al Aas on accepting Islam was so severely beaten by his father that his head was fractured.

However, regardless of all the torture, the believing men and women remained steadfast and not once did the Prophet tell them to retaliate. The strategy of combating the persecution, in this stage of the Da'wah, was by patience and not retaliation. The Muslims were few in number and were at a very early stage of the movement; retaliation could prove to be damaging for the cause of Islam and as the Qur'an reminds the Muslims:

$$أَمْ حَسِبْتُمْ أَن تَدْخُلُوا ٱلْجَنَّةَ وَلَمَّا$$
$$يَأْتِكُم مَّثَلُ ٱلَّذِينَ خَلَوْا مِن قَبْلِكُم مَّسَّتْهُمُ ٱلْبَأْسَاءُ وَٱلضَّرَّاءُ$$

Or do you think that you will enter Paradise without such
(trials) as came to those who passed away before you?
(Al Baqarah 2 : v 214)

Rule of Makkah is Offered

The Quraish were faced with a difficult situation. They had begun their opposition by ridicule, then propaganda, then compromise and now through persecution; yet Prophet Muhammad and the Muslims would not give up their cause. Utbah Ibn Rabiah was authorised to approach Prophet Muhammad with certain proposals: "If you want from your movement riches; we will collect such wealth for you that you will be the richest man in Makkah. If you want leadership; we will make you our chief and take no decision without your consent. If you want to become a ruler; we will make you our king. If you want women; we will provide you with the most beautiful women in Makkah. If you are under the influence of a jinn; we will pay the necessary expenses of curing you."

The Prophet had been offered the rule of Makkah by the Quraish, yet he declined it. Political power was not the aim of the Prophet.

His aim was to establish Islam in society so that Allah would be worshipped alone (thus political power is the means). The people of Makkah were not prepared to accept Allah as their Lord; of what benefit would it then have been if the Prophet was the ruler of Makkah?

The Prophet after listening to all the proposals recited to Utbah:

$$حمٓ ۝ وَٱلۡكِتَٰبِ ٱلۡمُبِينِ ۝ إِنَّا جَعَلۡنَٰهُ قُرۡءَٰنًا عَرَبِيًّا لَّعَلَّكُمۡ تَعۡقِلُونَ ۝ وَإِنَّهُۥ فِىٓ أُمِّ ٱلۡكِتَٰبِ لَدَيۡنَا لَعَلِىٌّ حَكِيمٌ ۝ أَفَنَضۡرِبُ عَنكُمُ ٱلذِّكۡرَ صَفۡحًا أَن كُنتُمۡ قَوۡمًا مُّسۡرِفِينَ ۝$$

Ha Mim. By the manifest Book (Qur'an). We verily, have made it a Qur'an in Arabic, that you may be able to understand.
And verily, it (the Qur'an) is in the Mother of the Book, before Us indeed Exalted, full of Wisdom. Shall we then take away the Reminder from you because you are people who transgress.
(Az Zukhruf 43 : v 1-5)

The Prophet recited up to verse thirteen whilst Utbah listened attentively. Utbah returned to the Quraish and when asked whether or not the Prophet had given an answer; he replied: "I have never heard such a recitation as this. By God it is neither poetry, nor magic, nor soothsaying. O People of Quraish! Accept my word and leave its responsibility to me. If the people of Arabia accept the message of Islam, you will be removed without any effort. But if he dominates over Arabia, his kingdom will be your kingdom and his power yours, and you will become the most fortunate of men through him." The Quraish laughed at Utbah claiming that he had also fallen under the spell of the Qur'an.

A second attempt was made on behalf of the Quraish by the leaders of the tribes, including Walid Ibn Al Mughira, Abu Jah Ibn Hisham and Abu Sufyan Ibn Harb. The offer of power, money and fame was repeated. The Prophet again explained: "My objective is quite different to what you speak of. I have not come to you with my call for the purpose of collecting wealth or desiring leadership over you. Allah has sent me to you as His Messenger and revealed to me His law *(Shari'ah)* and ordered me to warn you and give glad tidings. I have communicated His Message to you; if you accept what I have conveyed, you will benefit in this world as well as in the hereafter. If you reject, I shall wait patiently for that day when Allah will decide between you and me." The Quraish returned enraged and continued the persecution.

Migration to Abyssinia

The Prophet Muhammad had tolerated the abuses and occasional violence against him, but upon seeing the state of his companions, he decided to permit those followers, who mainly lacked tribal protection to migrate *(Hijrah)* to Abyssinia. He told them: "It would be better if you migrate to Abyssinia; there a king rules and in whose territory no-one is wronged. Stay there until Allah makes circumstances favourable for you to return."

In the fifth year of Prophethood, a group of eleven men and five women left for Abyssinia. They were headed by Uthman Ibn Affan *(Ameer)* and the group consisted of: Ruqayyah (the daughter of the Prophet and wife of Uthman), Abdur Rahman Ibn Awf, Uthman Ibn Mazum, Hatib Ibn Amr, Abu Sabara Ibn Umar, Amir Ibn Rabiah and his wife, Suhayl Ibn Bayda, Zubayr Ibn Al Awwam,

Abu Hudhaifah and his wife, Abu Salmah, Umm Saimah and Musab Ibn Umayr.

They were well received by Najashi (Negus) and were treated with justice. It was not long after that some of them returned to Makkah secretly whilst others entered through the protection of their supporters. The return of the group of believers from Abyssinia enraged the Quraish and they decided to persecute the Muslims more harshly. This led to the emigration of a second larger group to Abyssinia. In total there were eighty five men and woman in this group. Again Najashi welcomed them and promised them security and justice.

The Quraish decided to send two envoys, Abdullah Ibn Rabia and Amr Ibn Al Aas, with valuable gifts, to Najashi to expel the Muslims from Abyssinia. They succeeded in bribing the chiefs and priests but Najashi said that he could not decide the matter without hearing what the Muslims had to say in their defence. Thus the following day, the representatives of the Quraish and the Muslims were summoned before the king.

The representatives of the Quraish claimed that the Muslim refugees should be expelled from Abyssinia and handed over to them on the grounds that their leader had abandoned the religion of their forefathers and was preaching something contrary to their customs.

Jafar Ibn Abu Talib who spoke on behalf of the Muslims, sought permission from Najashi to question Amr Ibn Al Aas before presenting their case. Once the permission was granted, Jafar Ibn

Abu Talib asked Amr: "Are we slaves of any master that we have deserted and deserve to be sent back?" Amr was hesitant to answer the question but on Najashi's order he replied: "No, they are free men and women." "Have we escaped after murdering anyone so that we may be handed over to the relatives of the victims?" asked Jafar. "No, they have not shed a single drop of blood," answered Amr. Jafar then proceeded to his third question: "Have we escaped from paying any debts or have stolen property, if so we are prepared to compensate and repay the debts?" Amr replied: "No, they have not stolen anything nor do they owe anybody a single dirham."

Having displayed the moral uprightness of the Muslims, Jafar addressed the king: "O king! We were ignorant people and worshipped idols made out of our own hands. We oppressed our neighbours and brothers were fighting brothers. We killed our baby daughters thinking them to be of no use. We ate dead bodies and cheated the poor; then amidst us rose a man whose birth, nobility and integrity was well known amongst us. He called us to the worship of One Allah and taught us not to associate anything with Him. He taught us to speak the truth, refrain from bloodshed, to be merciful, safeguard the rights of our neighbours, forbade us to speak ill of women and mistreat orphans. He ordered us to offer prayer *(Salah)*, observe fasts *(Siyam)*, to give alms *(Sadaqah)* and to propagate this message *(Da'wah)*. We have believed in him as the Final Messenger of Allah and have also accepted his teachings. We renounced our bad habits and took Allah as our Lord; whereupon our people have become hostile and have persecuted us. Finding no safety among them, we have come to your country hoping you will protect us."

Najashi was very impressed by these words, however Amr cunningly interrupted and said: "But these people do not believe in Jesus the same way you do (son of God)." Najashi asked Jafar as to what Prophet Muhammad had said about Jesus. Amr replied: "Our Prophet has told us that Jesus is the servant and Prophet of God," and recited to him the story of the birth of Prophet Isa (Jesus); the surah (chapter of the Qur'an) brought tears to his eyes of Najashi and he exclaimed: "It seems that the words revealed to Jesus and the words revealed to Muhammad are from the same source. I am sure that Muhammad is the Prophet whose advent was prophesied by Jesus." He picked up a straw from the ground and said: "By God! Jesus is not different even by this straw from what you have said of him." He then returned the gifts of the Quraish and allowed the Muslims to live in Abyssinia with full protection.

Hamza Ibn Abdul Muttalib Accepts Islam

In Makkah whilst the oppression of the Muslims was ever increasing in intensity, new people were coming to the fold of Islam and important personalities from amongst the leaders of the Quraish were also attracted to Islam. One such person was Hamza Ibn Abdul Muttalib, the Prophet's uncle and one of the bravest men in Makkah.

It happened that the Prophet was seated one day near the Mount of Safa when Abu Jahl passed by and insulted the Prophet in a most degrading manner. The Prophet kept silent and did not utter a single word. A slave girl belonging to Abdullah Ibn Judah witnessed the incident and related it to Hamza, who was just returning from a hunting expedition. She said to him: "O Abu Nummrah! Would you have witnessed the pitiable condition when your nephew was abused by Abu Jahl. He was insulted very badly, yet your nephew remained silent." Hamza was deeply offended and went directly to Abu Jahl, who was sitting with others in the Ka'bah, and taking his bow, struck him with a violent blow to his face and said: "You have insulted my nephew. Will you insult him when I too follow his way and say what he says? Hit me back if you can!" The men of Banu Makhzum came to Abu Jahl's aid but he stopped them saying that he had indeed abused the Prophet Muhammad badly. From there, Hamza went to Darul Arqam and declared his acceptance of Islam at the hands of the Prophet.

Umar Ibn Al Khattab Accepts Islam

The leaders of the Quraish had now become increasingly worried at the growth of the movement in Makkah and by the protection provided by Najashi for the Muslims in Abyssinia. They were yet to be surprised by the conversion to Islam of one of their most prominent leaders - Umar Ibn Al Khattab.

Umar was not motivated by any material consideration in his opposition of Islam; rather he saw it as his duty to preserve the existing social structure. He decided the best way to hinder the progress of the movement of Islam was to eliminate it's leader: Prophet Muhammad. He decided to take the task on himself. On his way, he met Nuaym Ibn Abdullah one of his friends, who asked him why he was in an angry mood. Umar replied that he was intending to kill the man who had shattered the unity of the Quraish and insulted their ancestors. Nuaym told him: "By God, Umar! Your soul has deceived you; do you think that the Banu

Abdu Manaf would let you walk on this earth if you killed Muhammad? Why don't you look at your own house where your sister Fatimah and your brother-in-law Saeed Ibn Zayd have embraced Islam?" Umar was unaware of this and immediately rushed to his sister's house.

Upon approaching her house he heard the voice of Khabbab Ibn Al Aratt, reciting something. Khabbab heard the footsteps and hid behind a closet. Umar entered and demanded an explanation for what he had heard. Knowing that they had become Muslims he lunged at Saeed but Fatimah rushed to rescue her husband and received a blow on the head by Umar. In fright both Fatimah and Saeed cried out: "Yes, we have become Muslims and believe in One Allah and Prophet Muhammad as His Messenger. Do whatever you like but we will not abandon Islam."

A blood stained woman, and this too his own sister, in tears and declaring in such determination, conquered the rage of Umar and his heart softened. He asked to see what they were reading. Fatimah replied that first he must clean himself if he was to touch the words of Allah. Umar did so and began to read from the piece of paper that Khabbab was reading from :

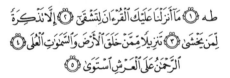

We have not sent down the Qur'an unto you to cause you distress.
But only as a Reminder to those who fear. A revelation from Him
Who has created the earths and the high heavens.
The Most Beneficent Who is established on the Throne.
(Ta-ha 20 : v 1-5)

Umar was fascinated by the verses he was reading and continued to read until he reached the verse :

$$إِنَّنِي أَنَا اللَّهُ لَا إِلَٰهَ إِلَّا أَنَا فَاعْبُدْنِي وَأَقِمِ الصَّلَوٰةَ لِذِكْرِي ﴿١٤﴾$$

Verily, I am Allah, there is no God except Me
So Worship Me and offer prayers perfectly for My Remembrance.
(Ta-Ha 20 : v 14)

Immediately he responded by asking Khabbab to take him to the Prophet so that he could attest the Truth and submit to Allah.

Khabbab took him to Darul Arqam where the Prophet was with his companions. As he was walking towards the house, his sword was swinging on his arm and thus when a companion, who was looking to see who was at the door, said: "It is Umar Ibn Al Khattab with his sword," Hamza replied: "Let him in, as a friend he is welcome; as an enemy, he will have his head chopped off by his own sword." Umar came and went to the Prophet and declared.

أشهد أن لا إله إلا الله وأشهد أنّ محمدا عبده و رسوله

I bear witness that there is no God but Allah and that Prophet Muhammad is His Servant and Messenger.
(Declaration of Faith)

He swore that the sword with which he had intended to kill Prophet Muhammad would now be used in the struggle for the dominance of Islam. He went immediately to the Ka'bah and in the presence of the leaders of the Quraish, declared himself a Muslim. For this, the Quraish attacked him and beat him severely until Aas Ibn Wayl gave him protection. Similarly he went to the arch enemy of Islam - Abu Jahl and declared his faith in Islam. Abu Jahl replied: "God's curse be upon you and your news."

The acceptance of Islam by Umar and Hamza raised the morale of the Muslims and their movement was strengthened. Such was the effect that the Muslims could now dare to pray openly at the Ka'bah. It was also significant that the conversion took place at a time when the forces of oppression working against the Muslims were at their peak.

Social and Economic Boycott

Every possible attempt had been made to crush the growth of the movement of Islam and all the attempts had failed; yet the Quraish were determined to continue in their struggle. At a meeting, the leadership of the Quraish decided to boycott Prophet Muhammad, his companions and the tribe of Banu Hashim. It was agreed that no-one was to have any relations with them, to stop all provisions reaching them, no inter-marriages were to be allowed and no food was to reach them until they handed over Prophet Muhammad with the permission to kill him. In the seventh year of the movement, all the tribes of Quraish joined together in this agreement to boycott Prophet Muhammad and his tribe; they put a notice to that effect on the Ka'bah.

The Muslims and other members of the tribe of Banu Hashim had to take refuge in a long narrow valley called the 'Shibi Abu Talib' on the outskirts of Makkah. This valley was a gateway, so narrow that a camel could only just pass through it. All the family members of the Prophet were confined in this except Abu Lahab.

For three full years, they suffered. They ate leaves, barks of trees, boiled and drank the juice of dried skins. The wailing of the children could be heard from a far distance. Surveillance was strict, thus only on certain occasions food was brought to them by sympathetic people like Hakim Ibn Hazam, Abul Bakhtari and Hashim Ibn Amr. However, they realised that the suffering was for the cause of Allah and his Prophet. Surely they would not go without being rewarded by Allah in the hereafter. All of them had a deep-rooted love for the Prophet *(Mahabbatur Rasul)* and knew that their suffering was not futile.

During the third year of the boycott, a move initiated by Hashim Ibn Amr, was made to bring it to an end. Hashim secured support from others and challenged the boycott agreement, but again Abu Jahl opposed it. However, the great majority of the Quraish agreed with Hashim and the boycott was ended with the Muslims returning to their homes.

When the Quraish went to remove the document they had hung upon the Ka'bah, they found its text eaten away by white ants leaving only the words: 'In the name of God our Lord'.

Death of Abu Talib

The year following the end of the boycott turned into a year of personal sorrow for the Prophet Muhammad. It was in this year, in the tenth year of Prophethood, that his uncle Abu Talib died. It was partially through his uncle's support, that the Islamic Movement had reached this stage and the Prophet's personal safety was secured.

Whilst Abu Talib lay dying on his death bed, the Quraish approached him and asked him to settle the dispute with his nephew. They said to him: "Take an understanding from him on our behalf and one from us on his behalf; so that he should have nothing to do with us, nor us with him." The Prophet was called, and upon hearing the demand of the Quraish said: "All I want is for you to testify that there is none worthy of worship besides Allah and to forsake all other objects of worship and acknowledge that I am the Messenger of Allah. If you accept, you will be masters of Arabia and the non-Arabs will be subjected to you." The Quraish were unwilling to accept this.

Prophet Muhammad had on numerous occasions invited Abu Talib to Islam, but his uncle would not accept the message. The Prophet was extremely disappointed but Allah reminded him:

إِنَّكَ لَا تَهۡدِى مَنۡ أَحۡبَبۡتَ وَلَٰكِنَّ ٱللَّهَ يَهۡدِى مَن يَشَآءُ وَهُوَ أَعۡلَمُ بِٱلۡمُهۡتَدِينَ ۝

Verily! You guide not whom you like, but Allah guides whom He wills and He knows best those who are guided.

(Al Qasas 28 : v 56)

The Prophet even invited his uncle to Islam on his death bed: "O My uncle! Say none has the right to be worshipped except Allah then I will be able to defend your case before Allah." Abu Jahl and Abdullah Ibn Umayyah, who were present amongst the Quraish said: "O Abu Talib! Will you leave the religion of Abdul Muttalib?" They kept on saying this to him till the last statement Abu Talib said before dying was: "I am on the religion of Abdul Muttalib." The Prophet even though he was distraught said: "I will keep on asking for Allah's forgiveness for you unless I am forbidden to do

85

so." It was not long after, that the prohibition came:

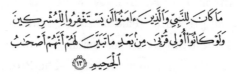

It is not proper for the Prophet and those who believe to ask Allah's
Forgiveness for the polytheists even though they may be of kin, after it has
become clear to them that they are the dwellers of the Fire
(i.e. died in a state of disbelief).
(Tawba 9 : v 113)

Death of Khadijah

The same year also witnessed the death of Khadijah. For twenty five
years she had been his counselor and constant source of support.
She whole-heartedly co-operated with the Prophet in all his efforts
and helped him financially; by sacrificing all her wealth. She
suffered many hardship but never wavered. The Prophet later said
of her: "She believed in me when no one else did; she embraced
Islam when people disbelieved me and she helped and comforted
me when there was none to lend me a helping hand." It is of no
surprise that she was given the title 'Mother of the Believers'.

Khadijah bore the Prophet several children. The first was named
Qasim (thus the Prophet was also known as Abul Qasim). Then
were born Tayyib and Tahir. All his sons died in their infancy.
Amongst the daughters, Ruqayyah was the eldest, then Zaynab,
Umm Kulthum and lastly Fatimah.

Prophet is Unprotected

The death of the Prophet's uncle had also resulted in the loss of support; the Prophet was now unprotected. A few days after the funeral, the Prophet went into the sanctuary of the Ka'bah and summoned the people to worship Allah. There was a sudden uproar and attack on him from every side. Harith Ibn Halah rushed to the spot and tried to save the life of the Prophet as a result of which he was killed.

It was common for the Prophet to see thorns thrown on the path by which he walked and dirt of animals thrown at him. On one occasion whilst he was prostrating in the Ka'bah, Abu Jahl asked his companion to bring a foetus of a she-camel and place it on the Prophet's back. Uqbah Ibn Abu Muyat was the person who obeyed the order and placed it on the Prophet's back. In the meantime Fatimah, the five year old daughter of the Prophet removed the filth from her father's back. The Prophet invoked the wrath of Allah upon them, especially Abu Jahl, Walid Ibn Utbah, Umayyah Ibn Khalaf and Uqbah Ibn Abu Muyat. He later said: "I lived amongst two of the worst type of neighbours: one of them was Abu Lahab and the other was Uqbah Ibn Abu Muyat."

On another occasion, whilst the Prophet was walking around the Ka'bah with Uthman Ibn Affan and a few other companions, Abu Lahab and his group of evil-doers laughed and made sarcastic remarks; when this happened three times in succession, the Prophet stopped and remarked: "You will never give up bad deeds until calamity falls on you from Allah." At this Abu Lahab and his companions shuddered. The Prophet went back to Uthman and the other companions and said: "I give you tidings that Allah shall certainly grant supremacy to His Faith, fulfil His Word and protect His Deen (Islam). The people whom you find powerful today shall be killed by your hands." In years to come, these words became a reality.

The wife of Abu Lahab was also involved in the persecution of the Prophet. She was the one who would regularly throw thorns in his way. Her activities led her to be cursed by Allah:

تَبَّتْ يَدَآ أَبِى لَهَبٍ وَتَبَّ ۝ مَآ أَغْنَىٰ عَنْهُ مَالُهُۥ وَمَا
كَسَبَ ۝ سَيَصْلَىٰ نَارًا ذَاتَ لَهَبٍ ۝ وَٱمْرَأَتُهُۥ
حَمَّالَةَ ٱلْحَطَبِ ۝ فِى جِيدِهَا حَبْلٌ مِّن مَّسَدِۭ ۝

Perish the two hands of Abu Lahab, and perish he.
His wealth and his children will not benefit him.
He will be burnt in a fire of blazing flames
And his wife too, who carries wood.
In her neck is a twisted rope of palm fibre.

(Masad 111 : v 1-5)

When these verses were revealed, the wife of Abu Lahab came out looking for the Prophet. Abu Bakr was sitting with the Prophet and when he saw her approaching, he said to the Prophet: "I wish for you to get aside as she is coming towards us; she may cause you harm." The Prophet replied: "There will be a screen set between me and her." She approached them, not seeing the Prophet, and said to Abu Bakr: "Your companion is reciting poetry against me," and left. The Prophet later explained that angels were screening him from her.

Once while the Prophet was praying in the Ka'bah, Uqbah Ibn Abu

Muyat made a rope, cast it around the neck of the Prophet and when the Prophet prostrated, he twisted it and pulled hard as to choke the Prophet's throat; but the Prophet continued with his prayer. In the meantime, Abu Bakr had arrived and pushed Uqbah back saying: "Do you slay a person because he says 'My Lord is Allah' and has come to you with clear signs?"

The Mission to Taif

The Prophet was disillusioned by the people of Makkah and realised that the land was not fertile for the establishment of Islam. Islam could only be established in a land where the people accepted Allah as their Lord and Sovereign and acknowledged him as the final Messenger of Allah. The people of Quraish had not only rejected the Message but had persecuted him and his companions. The Prophet had lost the support of his uncle and Abu Jahl had become the new chief of the Quraish. The situation forced him to seek the protection of some other tribe, so that he could continue the Da'wah of Islam. It was mainly for this purpose that he went to Taif, a city to the south east of Makkah.

He went to Taif with Zayd Ibn Haritha. Within Taif itself, power rested with three individuals: Abd Yalayl, Masood and Habib. The Prophet went to all three of them and explained to them his mission and the message of Islam. But all three refused to extend their protection and rejected the message of Islam. Abd Yalayl responded by saying: "I will tear the curtain of the Holy Ka'bah if God has made you His Prophet." Masood said: "Couldn't God find anybody else to send as His Prophet." Habib said: "I swear that I won't speak to you. It would be an insult for me to do so, if you are a true Prophet; and an insult to myself if you are false in your claim."

The response of the people of Taif was no better than that of the people of Makkah. Dispirited, the Prophet set out on the return journey, but still the people of Taif would not leave him alone; they made their dogs attack him and the children threw stones and hurled abuse at him such that his sandals were stuck to his feet by blood. Zayd tried to shield him with his blanket, but with no success. This continued for three miles and the Prophet began to pray to Allah: "O Allah! These people do not know that what I tell them is the Truth; they are doing this thinking it is right to do so. Be not angry with them and do not punish them but open their eyes and hearts to the Truth and help them to accept it." Such was the character of the Prophet, that even when they were driving him out of their city, he prayed to Allah to guide them and not to destroy them.

Some way out of town the Prophet decided to take refuge in a vineyard belonging to two brothers; Utbah and Shaybah, sons of Rabia. His body was covered with wounds but on his lips was the prayer: "O Allah! Help me! Do not leave me to defend myself. You are my Lord. To whom are You going to entrust me: to an unknown enemy who is bitter with me or to an enemy who has dominance over my affairs? Your protection is a great shield for me. I seek Your Will and Pleasure. No force or strength can come except from You."

In reply, Allah sent Jibrail asking the Prophet's permission to crush the people of Taif in between two mountains. The Prophet asked

Allah to forgive them with the hope that the next generation of Taif will accept Islam.

Utbah and Shaybah were disbelievers, but when they saw the Prophet's condition they wanted to help him. They sent Addas, their Christian slave with a few bunches of grapes to take to the Prophet. Addas did as he was told and when he presented the dates to the Prophet he was asked to join. As the Prophet took the grapes in his hand to eat, he recited the name of God. Addas enquired: "By God, it is unusual for people in this land to utter such words." The Prophet asked Addas where he came from and what his religion was. Addas replied that he was a Christian from Ninevah in Iraq. "So you are from the town of the good Jonah, son of Matthew," the Prophet observed. Addas asked in surprise: "How do you know Jonah?" The Prophet replied: "He was my brother and a Prophet like me". On hearing this Addas kissed the Prophet's head, hands and feet. When Addas returned to Utbah and Shaybah, they demanded an explanation. Addas replied: "O my masters! There is nothing better than this on the earth. He told me something that none but a Prophet could know."

The Prophet continued his journey from the vineyard and came to Nakhla. There he stayed for a few days before proceeding to Cave Hira and sent a word seeking the protection of Al Mutam Ibn Adi. Al Mutam agreed and sent his sons to bring the Prophet safely to the Ka'bah. He then announced to the Quraish that he had given protection to the Prophet.

In a single journey Prophet Muhammad was treated in four different ways by four different groups of people. One drove him out of their towns, pelting stones at him; a second extended hospitality to him; a third accepted Islam and the fourth provided him protection against the Quraish.

MI'RAJ: THE PROPHET MEETS ALLAH

The journey to meet Allah occurred on the 27th of Rajab in the tenth year of Prophethood. The Qur'an describes the purpose of the journey:

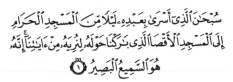

Glorified be the One who took His slave from a journey
by night from Al Masjid al Haram (Makkah) to the farthest Mosque (in
Jerusalem), the neighbourhood whereof We have blessed in order that We
might show him of Our signs. Verily, He is the All-Hearer, the All-Seer.

(Al Isra 17 : v 1)

On the night of the 27th of Rajab, whilst the Prophet was sleeping in the house of Umm Hani, daughter of Abu Talib, Jibrail came to the Prophet and took him to Hatim, a place near the Ka'bah. There he opened the Prophet's chest, took out his heart and washed it with the water of Zam Zam, in a golden basin filled with wisdom and mercy and put it back in its place. Jibrail then brought an animal known as the 'Buraq'; which resembled lightening in swiftness, was of a clear white colour, medium in size, smaller than a mule yet taller than a donkey and so quick, that in a single movement it could travel to the farthest limit of it's sight. Prophet Muhammad and Jibrail rode on the Buraq to Yathrib, where they descended and the Prophet offered two rakats of prayer. Jibrail then took the Prophet to Mount Sina and again the Prophet offered two rakats of prayer. The final place they stopped at before reaching Masjid Al Aqsa in Jerusalem was Baitul Laham, the birthplace of Prophet Isa.

At Masjid Al Aqsa, all the Prophets of Allah were present and awaiting the arrival of Prophet Muhammad. When he arrived he led the congregation in another two rakats of prayer. Jibrail then brought two jugs to the Prophet; one containing milk and the other containing wine. The Prophet chose the milk and refused the wine, to which Jibrail said: "You have been guided correctly to the fitrah (natural disposition) of Man, and so too will your people. Muhammad, wine is forbidden for you."

After the meeting with the Prophets, Jibrail took Prophet Muhammad to the heavens on the same Buraq. When they reached the first heaven the angel guarding it said: "Blessed be your arrival," and opened the door of the heaven. There he visited Prophet Adam, who welcomed him and saluted him. Prophet Adam then expressed faith in Muhammad's Prophethood and said: "You are welcome O Son and a Prophet!"

Angel Jibrail took him to the second heaven where he met with Prophet Isa and Yahya. Again he saluted them and they returned his salutation expressing faith in his Prophethood. From there, he went to the third heaven and met Prophet Yusuf; on the fourth met with Prophet Idris; on the fifth met Prophet Harun and on the sixth met with Prophet Musa. Whilst he was proceeding to the seventh heaven, Musa started weeping and on being asked the reason by Prophet Muhammad, he answered: "O Lord! Followers of this youth (Prophet Muhammad) who was sent after me will enter Paradise in greater numbers than my followers." The Prophet proceeded onto the seventh heaven, where he met with Prophet Ibrahim.

After the meeting with the Prophets he was taken to **Sidratul Muntaha** (a place above the heavens) and shown **Baitul Ma'mur**, a place directly above the Ka'bah in Makkah, which is circumambulated *(Tawaf)* by seventy thousand angels daily. An angel who had circumambulated the Ka'bah once would not have the opportunity to circumambulate again till the Day of Judgement. It was here that the Prophet received the revelation:

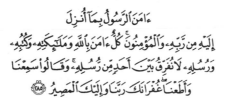

The Messenger believes in what has been sent down to him from his Lord and (so do) the believers. Each one believes in Allah, His Angels, His Books, and His Messengers. They say, "We make no distinction between one of His Messengers and another" and they say, "We hear and we obey. (we seek) Your Forgiveness, our Lord, and to You is the return.
(Baqarah 2 : v 285)

The Prophet was then shown Jannah and Jahannam and the scenes that will occur after the Day of Judgement. Jibrail then stopped and told the Prophet that he was incapable of going any further; another angel came with an animal called Raf Raf and took Prophet Muhammad into the Divine Presence of Allah.

When the Prophet saw Allah, he proclaimed:

التّحيّات لله والصّلوات والطّيّبات

All greetings, praises and goodness are for Allah.

Allah replied to this:

السلام عليك أيّها النّبيّ ورحمة الله وبركاته

Peace be upon you O Prophet, and the Mercy and Blessings of Allah
(be upon you too).

To which the Prophet replied:

السّلام علينا وعلى عباده الصّالحين

Peace be upon us and on the righteous servants of Allah.

Each of the angels who witnessed this, said:

أشهد أن لا إله إلا الله وأشهد أنَ محمدا عبده و رسوله

I bear witness that there is no God but Allah and I bear witness that
Muhammad is His Servant and Messenger.

Salah: Mi'raj of the Believers

Allah gave the Prophet some instructions and enjoined other
things, of which the most important was Salah - the daily prayers.
On his way back from the meeting with Allah, he met with Prophet
Musa again, who asked him regarding the nature of the orders
given by Allah. Upon hearing that fifty daily prayers had been
enjoined on the Muslims, Prophet Musa said: "I know the people
better than you because I had the hardest experience to bring Banu
Israil (Jews) to obedience. Your followers cannot put up with such
obligations; so return to your Lord and request Him to reduce the
number of prayers." The Prophet went back and requested Allah
and it was lowered to forty daily prayers. He returned to Musa and
had a similar discussion, and then returned to Allah for further
reductions. It was lowered again to thirty, then twenty, then ten

and came back to Musa again. Prophet Musa repeated the same advice and ultimately it was reduced to five daily prayers. When the Prophet came to Musa, the latter still repeated his advice, but this time the Prophet replied: "I feel ashamed of repeatedly asking Allah for reduction. I have surrendered and accepted the order of Allah." Allah then addressed the Prophet Muhammad: "I have decreed my obligation and have reduced the burden on my slaves, and I shall still reward a single good deed as if it were ten good deeds."

Hence, the five daily prayers were enjoined and were to be rewarded the same as fifty daily prayers. No other act of worship in Islam was to be given by Allah in this manner (of raising His Prophet to Him and enjoining the obligation of Salah). The Prophet later said: "The Salah is the Mi'raj of the believers."

Abu Bakr is Al Siddiq

When the Prophet returned to Makkah on the same night and the following day related his experience it led to different reactions. The disbelievers of the Quraish found it difficult to believe. With their materialistic outlook on life, they could not grasp this extraordinary event. They also found it a suitable opportunity to jeer at the Muslims and their belief; caravans take over a month to travel to Jerusalem, how could he have undertaken this journey in one night? They further asked the Prophet to give the description of Masjid al Aqsa and the city of Jerusalem. To their astonishment, he gave them the correct answer. He told them that two caravans were also on their way back and would arrive shortly in Makkah. The Muslims did not find it difficult to believe the journey. Surely Allah was the Creator of the heavens and the earth and everything between them; thus to take the Prophet to Him was not something impossible.

The disbelievers of the Quraish came to Abu Bakr who had not yet heard of the Mi'raj, and asked him whether he believed in the truth of the story of his friend Prophet Muhammad, that he had been to Jerusalem and had returned within a short span of the night. Abu Bakr enquired if the Prophet had actually said that. When they answered in the affirmative he replied: "Yes I am prepared to believe in what Prophet Muhammad says. The Prophet tells us that the Word of Allah comes to him directly from heaven to earth, at any hour by day or night and we believe in him. Isn't this a greater miracle than what you are doubting."

To Abu Bakr, belief in the Mi'raj was just like acceptance of the Prophethood of Muhammad. He was later honoured by Allah with the title 'As Siddiq' (one who verifies the truth) due to this act.

Others believed in the Prophet's journey when the two caravans returned and matched the exact description that the Prophet had said. The Qur'an tells them:

وَٱلنَّجْمِ إِذَا هَوَىٰ ۝ مَا ضَلَّ صَاحِبُكُمْ وَمَا غَوَىٰ ۝ وَمَا يَنطِقُ
عَنِ ٱلْهَوَىٰ ۝ إِنْ هُوَ إِلَّا وَحْيٌ يُوحَىٰ ۝ عَلَّمَهُ شَدِيدُ ٱلْقُوَىٰ ۝
ذُو مِرَّةٍ فَٱسْتَوَىٰ ۝ وَهُوَ بِٱلْأُفُقِ ٱلْأَعْلَىٰ ۝ ثُمَّ دَنَا فَتَدَلَّىٰ ۝
فَكَانَ قَابَ قَوْسَيْنِ أَوْ أَدْنَىٰ ۝ فَأَوْحَىٰ إِلَىٰ عَبْدِهِ مَا أَوْحَىٰ ۝
مَا كَذَبَ ٱلْفُؤَادُ مَا رَأَىٰ ۝ أَفَتُمَٰرُونَهُ عَلَىٰ مَا يَرَىٰ ۝

By the star when it goes down. Your companion has neither gone astray nor has erred. Nor does he speak of (his own) desire. It is only an inspiration that is inspired. He has been taught by One Mighty in power. He stood poised whilst he was in the highest part of the horizon. Then he approached and came loser. And was at a distance of two bow lengths or nearer. So did (Allah) convey the Inspiration to His slave. The (Prophet's) heart lied not regarding what he saw. Will you then dispute with him about what he saw?

(An Najm 53 : v 1-12)

Da'wah in Yathrib[1]

In Makkah, the Prophet continued with the Da'wah of Islam and invited tribe after tribe at assemblies, meetings and fairs. He preached to the pilgrims encamped at Makkah and Mina. He appealed to them to accept the sovereignty of Allah and leave all other objects of worship. Abu Lahab always followed the Prophet to such gatherings and prevented people from accepting Islam. He would call out to people: "O Men! This man wants to divide you. He insults our gods, al Lat and al Uzza, how can you listen to him?"

During the pilgrimage period, he had the opportunity to address tribes from Yathrib. They listened attentively to what the Prophet had to say and some of them decided to accept Islam. The

---

[1.] Yathrib was a town colonised by the Jews and remained under their control. The tribes Aws and Khazraj were also inhabitants of the town. Their ancestor was Qahtan of Persia. Two brothers named Aws and Khazraj came to Yathrib and settled there. From them descended the tribes of Aws and Khazraj. In the beginning they were independent of the Jews, but were forced later to make peace with them in a subordinate position. During this time a chief named Fatyun rose amongst the Jews and ordered that every newly married bride would have to share their first night with him. The Jews and the tribes of Aws and Khazraj obeyed this order, but later a warrior named Malik Ibn Ajla revolted and killed Fatyun and fled to Syria. When the ruler of Syria, Abu Jablah, heard the story of Fatyun, his army attacked the Jews and thus destroyed the Jewish power.The Aws and the Khazraj then became the dominant group. However, since they lacked unity amongst themselves, they fought many battles against each other. During the historic Battle of Basos, most of the leaders on both sides were killed and thus weakening their position. Hence the Jews again gained control. This was the situation at the time of the Prophet and later when the Prophet migrated to Yathrib, the name of the town was changed to Madinah.

responsibilities that fell upon those who accepted the message were then explained. The six people who accepted Islam on this occasion were: Abu Umama Asad Ibn Zarara, Abul Hasin Ibn Zihan, Awf Ibn Haris, Rafi Ibn Malik, Qutba Ibn Amir and Jabir Ibn Abdullah. They pledged to the Prophet that they would niether steal, nor commit adultery, nor kill their daughters, nor slander and would obey the Prophet at all times. They returned to Yathrib and began to spread the message of Islam in their communities, which were divided by tribal hatred.

The First Aqabah

The following year on the occasion of the Pilgrimage in Makkah, twelve people from Yathrib came in order to testify to the truth and accept Allah as their Lord. Ten were from the tribe of Khazraj and two from the tribe of Aws. They took allegiance **(Bay'ah)** and swore: "We will not worship anyone but Allah, we will not commit adultery, we will not kill our children and we will obey the Prophet in all his commands." This was the First Pledge of Aqabah.

The Prophet reminded them that if they were true to their pledge, they would receive Paradise as their reward. If they neglect it, then Allah would inflict punishment on them in this world or in the hereafter. Musab Ibn Umayr was sent by the Prophet with them to Yathrib so that he might teach them Islam and its doctrines. He lived in Yathrib with Abu Amama, preparing the ground for Islam through his relentless Da'wah. Individuals, families and tribes were accepting Islam with conviction in their belief in One Allah and His Messenger.

The Second Aqabah

The next Pilgrimage in the 12th year of Prophethood saw seventy four people (72 men and 2 women) from Yathrib go to Makkah to pledge their faith to Prophet Muhammad. The Prophet explained to them the responsibilities of a believer.

The delegation from Yathrib were willing to take the Prophet to Madinah and thus the centre of the movement was to transfer from Makkah to Yathrib (later to be called Madinah). The people in Madinah were willing to listen to the message of Islam, if not accept it. Hence the environment was non-hostile, suitable not only for Da'wah but also for the implementation of the rule of Allah *(Tatbeeq As Shari'ah Al Islamiyyah)*.

In Madinah, Abdullah Ibn Ubayy had stood out as a natural leader. The people decided to choose him as their king and thus a ceremony was planned in which Abdullah was to be crowned king of Madinah. However, at the Second Aqabah, the people of Madinah upon accepting Islam, realised that the person to reign and rule their society should not be Abdullah Ibn Ubayy but Prophet Muhammad.

The people of Madinah were requesting the Prophet to come to Madinah with them when Abbas Ibn Ubadah Ibn Nadla remarked: "O People of Khazraj! Do you know the significance of the pact you are entering into? By bringing him to Madinah you will be obliged to fight against all his enemies; your properties will be in danger. Your lives will be endangered. If you fear any of these, leave him now, but if you think you can carry out that which is expected of you, then undertake this heavy responsibility." The people said with one voice: "We accept this even if it means the loss of our property and our lives. But O Messenger of Allah, if we remain steadfast what will we gain?" "Paradise" was the reply, then they stretched out their hands and took the pledge in the following words: "We will all obey you O Prophet of Allah, in all sets of circumstances: in plenty as well as scarcity, in ease or hardship, in joy as well as in sorrow. We will speak the truth and never wrong anyone and in the Cause of Allah, we fear none."

Abul Haytham Ibn Al Tayyihan wanted assurance that if Allah granted the Prophet authority and victory, he would remain with the people of Madinah. The Prophet replied: "I will always remain with you. Your blood will be my blood. I will be with you in life and death. Your cause will be my cause. I will fight whom you fight and make peace with whom you make peace." The People of Madinah needed no further assurance.

The Prophet then selected twelve deputies who were to return back to Madinah to their tribes and to organise the Da'wah of Islam. The deputies *(nuqaba)* consisted of: Uzaid Ibn Hasid, Abul Hasim, Sa'd Ibn Khasima, Ibn Zara, Sa'd Ibn Rabiu, Abdullah Ibn Rawah, Sa'd Ibn Ubaydah, Mizar Ibn Amar, Barra Ibn Marur, Abdullah Ibn Amr, Ubaydah Ibn Samid and Rafi Ibn Malik. The appointment of these Nuqaba heralded the start of the construction of a new social order.

The event of the Second Aqabah had taken place secretly and thus at first, the Quraish were unaware of the new development of the Prophet's movement. Later, when they became aware they pursued the caravan returning to Madinah and managed to capture two of the Muslims, of whom one escaped and the other, Sa'd Ibn Ubaydah, was taken to Makkah and tortured.

HIJRAH: MIGRATION TO MADINAH

Makkah proved to be hostile to the message of Islam and its people had also persecuted the Prophet and the companions. Nevertheless, the Prophet had been able to lay the foundations of the movement in Makkah through Da'wah (preached the message of Islam), Jama'ah (organised those who responded to the call) and Tarbiyyah (trained them for the struggle).

In the meantime, the Quraish had renewed their persecution and the Prophet had been given implicit permission to allow his companions to migrate to Madinah. Abu Salmah was the first person to migrate to Madinah. He was later followed by his wife, Amir Ibn Rabia and his wife Layla, daughter of Abu Hathima, Abu Ahmad Ibn Jash and Abdullah. Within a short space of time, several quarters of the city had become deserted. Abu Jahl remarked sadly: "What has our cousin gained? He has disrupted our society, destroyed our unity and created dissension amongst us." For two months, the migration continued until most of the Muslims had migrated. Amongst those left behind in Makkah were the Prophet, Abu Bakr and Ali Ibn Abu Talib. The Quraish, alarmed by the new situation, decided to eliminate Prophet Muhammad, for if he were to migrate as well, it would make their task to impede the spread of Islam that much more difficult. They all gathered at the public hall called Darun Nadwa to consult on the method of eliminating the Prophet. Several people proposed that the Prophet should be confined in a house with an iron gate, but this was rejected. Others proposed that a person should be appointed to assassinate him; but this also was rejected on the grounds that the killing by one man would expose him and his family to revenge. Finally, Abu Jahl proposed that a group of young men from each tribe, armed with swords, should strike at the same time so that the responsibility of the Prophet's blood would be shared by all of the tribes and it would be impossible for revenge to take place. This proposal was unanimously accepted and preparations were made to execute the plan. However, Allah had informed the Prophet and as the Qur'an later reminded him:

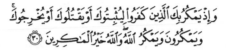

And (remember) when the disbelievers plotted against you
to imprison you, or to kill you, or to expel you (from
Makkah); they were planning and Allah too was planning,
and Allah is the Best of the Planners.

(Al Anfal 8 : v 30)

Thus on the appointed night the young men surrounded the Prophet's house and waited till morning for him to come out. The Prophet left the house and Allah took away the sight of the young men, so that they could not see the Prophet. He proceeded and taking a handful of dust, sprinkled it over their heads and recited the opening verses of Surah Yasin up to:

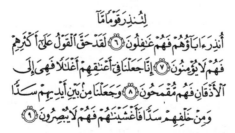

In order that you may warn a people whose forefathers were not warned, so
they are heedless. Indeed the word (of punishment) has proved true

against most of them, so they will not believe. Verily we have put on their
necks iron collars reaching to the chins, so that their heads are forced up.
And we have put a barrier before them, and
We have covered them up, so that they cannot see.

(Yasin 36 : v 6-9)

The Prophet had asked Ali to occupy his bed without any fear and told him to return some valuables, which people had kept with him, to their respective owners. Such was the stupidity of the Quraish, that they rejected the Truth; yet their faith in the character of Prophet Muhammad was never in doubt.

The Prophet proceeded to the house of Abu Bakr and informed him that Allah had commanded them to leave for Madinah. Abu Bakr shed tears of joy; he had been longing to migrate with the Prophet and now the time had come. He had already prepared two camels and offered them to the Prophet as a gift. The Prophet insisted on buying, and bought one of the camels.

As they were leaving the city of Makkah, the Prophet recalled the time he had spent in Makkah and casting his eyes towards the Ka'bah said: "By Allah, you are the most sacred place in the sight of Allah and I would have never left you if I was not forced to leave." The route was chosen by the Prophet himself and Abdullah Ibn Urayqat was hired as a guide. They travelled southwards and took refuge in a Cave in Mount Thawr. Here they remained for three nights. Amir Ibn Fuhayra would take his goats to the cave at night to supply them with milk. Abdullah Ibn Abu Bakr also visited the cave to inform them of the situation in Makkah.

In Makkah, the youth of the Quraish, who had kept an all night vigil were furious and baffled when they found that the Prophet had left, leaving Ali Ibn Abu Talib. The Quraish sent horsemen in the pursuit of the Prophet and announced a reward of one hundred camels to anyone who could capture the Prophet.

Attempts to Capture the Prophet

The Quraish had sent horsemen in every direction to capture the Prophet. One group of horsemen reached to the mouth of the Cave where the Prophet and Abu Bakr were hiding. Abu Bakr was frightened that they may look into the cave. Upon noticing the fright on Abu Bakr's face, the Prophet said: "O Abu Bakr, what do you think of those two with whom Allah is the third?" Whilst the horsemen were at the mouth of the cave, miraculously a spider had woven its web across the entrance of the cave. The horsemen decided that no one could enter the cave without breaking the web and returned to Makkah. Describing the scene in the cave the Qur'an says:

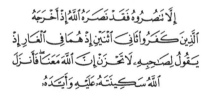

If you help him (Muhammad) not (it does not matter), for Allah did indeed
help him when the disbelievers drove him out, the second of the two, when
they (Muhammad and Abu Bakr) were in the cave, and he said to his
companion (Abu Bakr) "Be not sad, surely Allah is with us." Then Allah sent
down his tranquillity upon him, and strengthened him.

(Tawba 9:v 40)

After three days, Prophet Muhammad, Abu Bakr, Ibn Fuhayr (servant of Abu Bakr), and Abdullah Ibn Urayqah (he had not yet embraced Islam but was trusted by Abu Bakr and hired as a guide) started their journey again towards Madinah, by the longer route along the seashore.

The offer of one hundred camels by the Quraish tempted a few individuals to capture Prophet Muhammad; one such person was Suraqa Ibn Jushum. On hearing information that a group of four people had been located on a specific route, he decided to pursue the group. On his way, his horse stumbled and fell to the ground. He decided to draw a lot to see whether he should continue the pursuit or not; as was the Arab custom. The lots fell on returning back, but the reward of a hundred camels prevented him; thus the lust for material wealth made him resume the pursuit.

Once more, as he got close to the Prophet and Abu Bakr, the feet of his horse stuck to the dust and it stumbled. When it happened for a third time he realised this was a warning from Allah because of his evil intentions. He apologised and repented to the Prophet. He surrendered his weapons to the Prophet, who refused to take them, and appealed for a promise of safety. The Prophet accepted his repentance and when asked by Suraqa Ibn Jushum, he gave him a written agreement of the promise of safety. Suraqa then hurried back to Makkah and attempted to foil the plan of the other groups of horsemen who were intending to capture the Prophet. It was also during this outwardly desperate situation that the Prophet told Suraqa: "O Suraqa! How happy will you feel when the bracelets of the Emperor of Persia will be on your hands."

Barida Aslomi was another warrior who had decided to capture the Prophet with the sole intention of obtaining the reward. He set out with seventy horsemen and when he reached the Prophet, his heart changed and when the Prophet invited him to Islam, he accepted.

The Prophet and the others continued the journey till they reached a place owned by Umm Ma'bad Al Khuzaiyah. She was a well respected and generous lady, who sat at her tent with a carpet laid out so that she might be able to welcome passing travellers. Tired and thirsty, Prophet Muhammad and his companions rested there. Umm Ma'bad told them that the flocks were on the fields and the goat standing nearby was dry of milk. The Prophet touched the udders of the goat reciting the name of Allah and milk came pouring out. He offered it first to Umm Ma'bad and shared the rest with his companions.

After they had bid farewell, Abu Ma'bad returned and his wife related the whole incident. Abu Ma'bad asked her to give a description of the man, to which she replied: "His stature was neither too small nor too big. He had black attractive eyes and finely arched eyebrows. His hair was shiny black and curled. He wore a long garment and his expression was very sweet and distinct. His voice was commanding and his speech was marked by truth and sincerity, devoid of any malice, hatred or falsehood."

Abu Ma'bad realised that this was Prophet Muhammad; he decided to accept Islam along with his wife. They immediately decided to migrate to Madinah and on the way met Zubayr who welcomed them and helped them.

Arrival at Quba

The news that the Prophet had left Makkah reached the people in Madinah, and they were eagerly awaiting his arrival. The people would daily climb the roofs and trees hoping to witness his arrival but they would return because of the unbearable heat of the midday sun.

On one such day, after they had returned home; a Jew who caught a glimpse of approaching travellers shouted out: "O You People! The Prophet whom you have been waiting for has come." The call was immediately taken up by men, women and children who rushed into the streets. The day was the eighth of Rabiul Awwal in the thirteenth year of Prophethood.

The Prophet arrived and stayed with Khulthum Ibn Haddam, a chief of the tribe of Amr Ibn Awf in Quba, three miles away from Madinah. Many of the early emigrants also rested at his house on their way to Madinah. During his stay at Quba, which lasted for fourteen days, he was joined by Ali.

The Prophet's stay in Quba saw the establishment of the first mosque in the history of Islam. He himself participated in the construction of the mosque.

The first five daily prayers in congregation were also performed at his Mosque. At a nearby valley of Banu Salim the Prophet performed the first Friday Prayer *(Jumu'ah)* and addressed the Muslims saying:

"Praise be to Allah. I seek His forgiveness, guidance and help and declare my faith in the Oneness of Allah. Whoever obeys Allah and the Prophet will find righteousness and he who disobeys is astray and in gross error. I order you to fear Allah and avoid that which He has commanded you to avoid and enjoin what He has told you to enjoin. Your relation with Allah, whether seen (public) or unseen (private) should be based on Truth. This can be achieved by making your prime objective, seeking the pleasure of Allah. Such a course of life will give you honour and fame in this world and it will help you in the next world. Fear Allah and do not show any slackness in your obedience to Allah. He has revealed the Book (Qur'an) so that falsehood can be distinguished from the Truth. Look upon His enemy as yours. No power is of any use to anyone except the Power of Allah. Remember Allah as much as you can and live a life for the next world. If your relation with Allah is based on sincerity, then Allah will save you from evils; therefore keep your relation with Allah intact for He is The Greatest and The All Mighty." Henceforth, this place became to be known as Masjid al Jumu'ah (Friday Mosque).

Reception at Yathrib

The Prophet arrived in Madinah to see men, women and children of all ages gathered in the streets singing and expressing their gladness and joy. The women sang:

طلع البدر علينا من ثنيّات الوداع   وجب الشّكر علينا ما دعا لله داع

أيّها المبعوث فينا جئت بالأمر المطاع   جئت شرّفت المدينة مرحبا يا خير داع

O the White Moon rose over us, from the Valley of Wada

111

And we owe it to show gratefulness, where the call is to Allah.
O you who were raised amongst us, coming with a word to be
obeyed, you have brought to this city nobleness,
Welcome! Best caller to God's way.

The young girls beating their drums sang:

We are the daughters of Banu Najjar
Welcome to you O Muhammad!

This was the first time that the Prophet had been welcomed in such
a manner; and also the first time that the people of Madinah had
welcomed anybody in this manner.

People from all the tribes invited the Prophet to stay with them.
However, the Prophet pointed to his camel and replied: "The
camel is under the command of Allah; wherever it stops, that will
be my place of stay." The camel moved towards the houses
inhabited by Banu Najjar and knelt down before the house of Abu
Ayyub, who was finding it difficult to contain his joy. The Prophet
stayed at his house for seven months.

Mosque: Centre of the Islamic Society

The first action that the Prophet carried out after his arrival in
Madinah was to order the construction of a mosque, which was to
act as the focal point of society. The site was acquired by Abu
Ayyub who paid the price of ten gold coins to its two orphan
owners who later donated the money back. It was also the site on
which Qaswa, the Prophet's camel, had stopped.

The construction of the mosque was started by levelling the ground and clearing some palm trees. It was to consist of the mosque itself and two apartments for the Prophet and his family. The Prophet also worked alongside the Muslims and encouraged them. As they worked in the heat of the sun, the Prophet Muhammad sang to encourage the Muhajirun and the Ansar:

اللّهمّ إنّ الأجرَ أجرُ الآخرة فارحم الأنصار والمهاجرة

اللّهمّ إنّ الخيرَ خيرُ الآخرة فانصر الأنصار والمهاجرة

O Allah, verily the real reward is the reward of the Hereafter
So have mercy on the Helpers and Emigrants.
O Allah, there is no benefit except the benefit of the Hereafter
So, Help the Helpers and Emigrants.

The Prophet's presence and his participation made them even more joyful and thus expressing their joy, they sang :

لئن قعدنا والنّبيّ يعمل فذلك منّا العمل المظلل

If we sit back while the Prophet laboured.
That would be our most misguided action.

The structure of the mosque was extremely simple. The foundation was made with stones and the walls with grey mud bricks. The roof was covered by the branches of palm trees. The rest of the mosque was an open, roofless courtyard. The site of the plot was thirty five by thirty yards and had three doors. The eastern door was reserved for the Prophet's household and called *'Bab al Nisa'*; the southern door was a public entrance and the door on the west was called *'Bab al Rahman'*.

In the roofed portion of the mosque, a place was reserved for the **Ahlus Suffah** (people of the porch). These were the companions of the Prophet who had neither families nor homes. They devoted their entire life and energy to the study of Islam and the Qur'an. They were also responsible for the Da'wah in Madinah.

The role of the mosque was not merely limited to a place of salah; rather it was the centre of the Islamic society of Madinah. It was a court, a consultation centre, a hall, an official guest house, a hospital and a place of learning the Deen of Islam.

It was during the first month, whilst the mosque was still being built, that the Muslims suffered a great loss in the death of Abu Umama Asad Ibn Zarara; the first man to give bay'ah to the Prophet at Aqabah. It was he who had been the host of Musab and worked closely with him during the year between the two pledges of Aqabah.

It was at the funeral of Abu Umama that the second meeting between Salman the Persian and the Prophet, took place. Another man who embraced Islam at this time was a Jewish Rabbi of Banu Qaynuqa, Husayn Ibn Sallam. He came to the Prophet in secret and pledged allegiance to him; the Prophet renamed him as 'Abdullah'.

As Sahifah: First Constitution of the World.

The next important task to which the Prophet directed his full attention was the establishment of friendly relations between the Muslims and the non-Muslims (mainly consisting of Jews) and formulating rules and principles upon which the Islamic Society of Madinah was to be governed. This was the first political agreement between the Muslims and non-Muslims as well as being the first written constitution of the world. The Treaty was known as the Sahifah and it was made between Prophet Muhammad, the Muhajirun, the Ansar and the various clans and tribes of the Jews of Madinah. Some of the provisions of the Sahifah are as follows:

1. In the name of Allah, the Most Compassionate the Most Merciful. This is a document written by Muhammad the Prophet (governing the relations) between the believers and the Muslims from Quraish and Yathrib, and those who followed and joined them and strove with them, and those who are with the men of the faith (Jews).

2. They form one group to the exclusion of other people.

3. The God-fearing believers shall be against whoever rebels or the one who seeks to spread injustice, or sin or aggression or spread enmity between the believers; even if he is a son of one of them.

4. In peace and war all the believers must stand together.

5. The believers are supported by each other. The Jew who follows us is surely entitled to our support and the same equal rights as us. He shall not be wronged nor shall his enemies be assisted.

6. A believer shall not kill another believer, nor shall support an unbeliever against a believer. The protection of Allah is one and is equally extended to the humblest of believers.

7. The peace of the believers is indivisible. No separate peace shall be made when believers are fighting in the way of Allah.

8. It shall not be lawful for a believer who agrees with this document and believes in Allah and the Day of Judgement to help a criminal nor give him refuge.

9. Those who give him refuge and assistance shall have the Curse and Anger of Allah on the Day of Judgement.

10. Whoever is convicted of deliberately killing a believer without a righteous cause, shall be liable to retaliation, unless the relatives are satisfied (with the money paid in compensation for the killing).

11. Whenever you have a disagreement amongst you it must be referred to Allah and to Prophet Muhammad.

12. The Jews must contribute to the cost of war so long as they are fighting with the believers.

13. The Jews of Banu Awf are one community with the believers. They shall profess their religion and the Muslims theirs. The freedom and lives of the Jews shall be protected except those who act unjustly. The same applies to the tribes of Banu Najjar and the other tribes.

14. No-one shall go forth to war except with the permission of Muhammad; but this shall not hinder anyone from seeking lawful revenge.

15. The Jews shall be responsible for their expenditure; the Muslims for theirs, but if attacked, each shall come to the assistance of the other. The condition must be one of mutual advice and consultation.

16. Yathrib shall be a sanctuary for the people of this document.

17. No-one shall give protection of person and property to the Quraish and their helpers.

18. Allah approves and is pleased with the piety and goodness of this document.

19. This document shall not constitute any protection for the unjust and oppressors.

Many other provisions were also laid down and later all the parties agreed to abide by the document.

ESTABLISHMENT OF THE FIRST ISLAMIC STATE

The Sahifah laid down the foundations of an Islamic State *(Ad Dawlah al Islamiyyah)* in Madinah. It illustrated the Prophet's unparalleled political vision and his position as head of the Islamic State of Madinah. It was impossible for the Muslims to establish the social order of Islam without a state of their own. The primary aim of the migration to Madinah was the establishment of Islam in society.

The birth of an Islamic State in Madinah enabled its inhabitants to worship Allah in totality, as Islam was at the helm of authority and the Rule of Allah was to be implemented in society. The final political, legal and judicial authority was given to the Messenger of Allah.

It also provided a base to initiate and organise the Da'wah of Islam in other parts of Arabia.

The Islamic Brotherhood

The organisation of brotherhood *(Ukhuwwah)* amongst the Ansar and the Muhajirun was the next task. Surely no state could function and flourish without social harmony and organised, collective efforts of its inhabitants; the Islamic State of Madinah was no exception.

The small population of Madinah had to absorb hundreds of migrants, who had left their homes and relatives, and had no source of livelihood. The Prophet solved the problem by assigning to each

Ansar, a Muhajir brother and who was made responsible for his welfare. Hence, Muadh Ibn Jabal (Ansari) was responsible for Jafar Ibn Abu Talib (Muhajir), Kharijah Ibn Zayd was responsible for Abu Bakr As Siddiq, Itban Ibn Malik was responsible for Umar Ibn Al Khattab, Saeed Ibn Muadh Al Rabi was responsible for Abdur Rahman Ibn Awf and Aws Ibn Thabit was responsible for Uthman Ibn Affan; and so forth.

The Prophet, in his wisdom, did not select any specific brother from a clan; thus avoiding the resurrection of old clan rivalries. The members of his house consisted of Ali Ibn Abu Talib, Hamzah Ibn Abdul Muttalib, Abdullah Ibn Masud, Zubayr Ibn Al Awwam and Zayd Ibn Harith. It was also during this time that the Prophet married A'isha, the daughter of Abu Bakr, whilst he was living with Sawdah, whom he married after the death of Khadijah.[1]

The brotherhood and love amongst the Muhajrun and the Ansar, was so close that one example would suffice to demonstrate the closeness between them. Sa'd Ibn Sabi (Ansari), the richest man amongst the Ansar offered his brother Abdur Rahman Ibn Awf, half of his wealth and property. He even offered to divorce one of his two wives so that Abdur Rahman could get married. However, Abdur Rahman matched Sa'd in his nobility by refusing to take anything. He simply asked Sa'd to direct him to the market so that he could make his fortune with his own hands.

[1.] The Prophet later married Hafsa bint Al Khattab, Zaynab, Umm Salamah, Zaynab bint Jahsh, Juwayriah, Maymuna and Safiyyah. The marriages were either based on compassion i.e. they had no family or for the sake of building relationships and thus having access to different tribes, so that the message of Islam could be propagated and heads of rival tribes could be reconciled with each other.

The relationship between the Ansar and Muhajirun was not merely a temporary emotional expression; it developed and strengthened to the extent that if either of the two brothers passed away, his property was inherited by his other brother in Islam. This practice continued until its abrogation:

And those who believed afterwards, and emigrated and
strove hard along with you (in the Cause of Allah) they are of you. But kindred
by blood are nearer to one another regarding inheritance in the decree ordained
by Allah. Verily Allah is the All Knower of everything.

(Anfal 8 : v 75)

The establishment of this brotherhood, was unique in the history of the world: long-lasting tribal rivalries and hatred for one another was replaced by the principles of love *(Mahabbah)*, co-operation *(Ta'awun)* and collectiveness *(Jama'ah)*. As the Qur'an says:

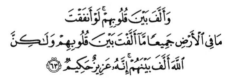

And He has united their hearts. If you had spent all that is in the earth, you
could not have united their hearts, but Allah has united them. Certainly He is
All Mighty, All Wise.

(Anfal 8 : v 63)

Establishment of Salah

The Muslims whilst in Makkah had offered the five obligatory daily prayers; but the prayers were implemented in the congregational form *(Jama'ah)* in Madinah. Upon completion of the construction of the mosque; the establishment of salah was of utmost priority. The Prophet was given political authority, not for worldly benefits and status but as the Qur'an explains:

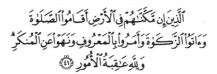

Those who if We give them power in the land (they) order the establishment of prayer, the paying of Zakah and they enjoin good and forbid evil (i.e. they make the Qur'an as the law of their country in all the spheres of life).
And with Allah rests the end of (all) matters.
(Al Hajj 22 : v 41)

The Prophet led the five daily congregational prayers and ensured that all the Muslims of Madinah were attending them. He explained to them that the purpose of salah was spiritual training and a tool to avoid evil *(munkar)*. The reward was to be twenty seven times higher than that of the salah offered individually. Such was the importance that on one occasion when there was a significant absence of Muslims during a congregational prayer, the Prophet remarked: "I wish I might appoint one of you to lead the prayer, and then I would venture outside to the houses of those absentees and set their houses ablaze; if it were not for the women and children."

Even the excuses and difficulties of a blind man was not a valid argument in the sight of the Prophet. He replied to the blind man: "It is better for you even if you have to come to the mosque crawling." The Prophet constantly reminded the Muslims that he who establishes salah; establishes Islam, but whoever abandons it; destroys Islam.

Adhan: The Call to Salah

There arose a problem regarding the best way to call the Muslims to the mosque for prayers. Several suggestions were put forward and discussed in a consultation meeting *(Shura)*. The blowing of a horn was proposed, but rejected as this was the method used by the Jews to call their people to the synagogue. Striking a bell was another proposal put forward but again this was rejected as it was the method of the Christians. The discussions continued until one day, Abdullah Ibn Zayd came to the Prophet Muhammad and said that he had a dream in which he had seen a man dressed in green, holding a wooden clapper. He asked the man: "Would you sell me your clapper, in order to call the people to salah?" The man replied: "Should I not show you a better way than this? Say:

الله أكبر الله أكبر الله أكبر الله أكبر

أشهد أن لا إله إلا الله أشهد أن لا إله إلا الله

أشهد أن محمّدا رسول الله أشهد أن محمّدا رسول الله

حيّ على الصّلاة حيّ على الصّلاة

حيّ على الفلاح حيّ على الفلاح

الله أكبر الله أكبر

لا إله إلا الله

Allah is the Greatest, Allah is the Greatest
Allah is the Greatest, Allah is the Greatest
I bear witness that there is no God but Allah
I bear witness that there is no God but Allah
I bear witness that Muhammad is the Messenger of Allah
I bear witness that Muhammad is the Messenger of Allah
Come to Prayer, Come to Prayer
Come to Success, Come to Success
Allah is the Greatest, Allah is the Greatest
There is no God but Allah.

(Adhan: Call to Prayer)

The Prophet replied: "Surely your dream is a vision from Allah. Go to Bilal and tell him to call to prayer accordingly." When Umar Ibn Al Khattab heard Bilal calling the Adhan, he came out of his house and told him that he had seen exactly the same vision himself. The Prophet replied: "Allah be praised for that."

Change of the Qiblah

The Qiblah (direction of prayer) was at first, towards Jerusalem; the same direction the Jews faced, but the relationship between the Jews and the Muslims weakened because of the propaganda of hatred initiated by the Jews against the Muslims. The Muslims could not bear to face towards Jerusalem and thus have something in common with the Jews. The Prophet along with the companions were awaiting revelation from Allah; as the Qur'an describes:

$$قَدْ نَرَىٰ تَقَلُّبَ وَجْهِكَ فِى ٱلسَّمَآءِ$$

$$فَلَنُوَلِّيَنَّكَ قِبْلَةً تَرْضَىٰهَا فَوَلِّ وَجْهَكَ شَطْرَ ٱلْمَسْجِدِ$$

$$ٱلْحَرَامِ وَحَيْثُ مَا كُنتُمْ فَوَلُّوٓا۟ وُجُوهَكُمْ شَطْرَهُۥ$$

Verily! We have seen the turning of your face towards heaven. Surely We shall
turn you to a Qiblah that shall please you so turn your face in the direction of
Masjid Al Haram (in Makkah) And
wheresoever you people are, turn your faces in that direction.

(Baqarah 2 : v 144)

When the revelation came the Muslims were engaged in prayers,
but immediately turned their faces to the direction of the Ka'bah.
They were overjoyed and relieved but the Jews were annoyed; they
asked for a rational reason for changing the Qiblah from Jerusalem
to the Ka'bah.[1] It was unnecessary for the Prophet to answer:

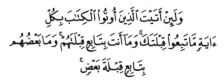

And even if you were to bring to the people of the Scriptures (Jews and
Christians) all the Ayat (proof, evidence, signs, verses) they would not follow
your Qiblah. Nor are you going to follow their Qiblah. And they will not
follow each other's Qiblah.

(Baqarah 2 : v 145)

[1.] It is interesting to note that whilst at Makkah, the Prophet was ordered to pray facing Jerusalem;
but due to a strong Jewish element in Madinah, he was ordered to turn towards Makkah. It is known
that the Ka'bah at that time was filled with three hundred and sixty idols; yet the Prophet was told
to face that direction in Salah. This illustrates that the purpose of the Prophets mission was not
simply the abolition and destruction of certain man-made idols or systems; rather it was for a more
comprehensive aim of transforming the society from the worship of man-made idols and systems to
the worship of One Allah.

The Jews further argued that Muhammad, by changing the direction of prayer, has opposed all other earlier Prophets. If he was a genuine Prophet he would have never done that. The hypocrites also remarked that the change of Qiblah meant that the Prophet had erred earlier and thus they were not sure which way to face.

The Jews had a faint hope that in the course of time, the Muslims would return to the religion of Musa, but the change of the Qiblah, shattered this hope and firmly established the uniqueness of Islam.

Betrayal of the Jews

When the Jews had concluded the agreement of the Sahifah with the Prophet, they were under the impression that the strength of the Muslims would weaken and soon they would be in a dominant position. However, they became anxious and developed a deep sense of hatred for the Muslims, when they found Islam entering their own households. A few common Jews entered Islam, but then leaders such as Husayn Ibn Sallam and Abu Qubays Ibn Abu Anas started accepting Islam.

The Jewish opposition, unlike the opposition of the Quraish, was sinister and treacherous. Open opposition was impossible because of the provisions of the Sahifah; they resorted to treacherous methods of spreading rumours, sowing discontent amongst the Muslims, making a mockery of Islam and asking futile questions to occupy the minds of the Muslims. On one such instance, after the death of Abu Amama, the Jews started to spread a propaganda that if Prophet Muhammad was really appointed by God, he would not have been deprived of such a valuable person. The Prophet replied to this by saying: "The death of Abu Amama was inevitable; for before Allah's will, neither can I avoid death nor prevent the death of my companion."

The opposition also took form in trying to involve the Prophet in irrelevant discussions in order to deviate the minds of the Muslims. On one occasion a group of Jewish Rabbis came to the Prophet telling him that they wanted to ask four question; and if he could satisfactorily answer their questions they would accept Islam. The four questions were:

1. Why does a child take after his mother when it is from the seed of the father?

2. Describe to us the condition of your sleep.

3. Prophet Jacob had prohibited for himself many things: what were they and why did he prohibit them?

4. Who is it that brings revelation to you?

The questions, absurd and strange as they may seem, were answered by the Prophet and not once did the Rabbis object. But when the Prophet, in answering the last question mentioned that it was Angel Jibrail, they said: "But O Muhammad! Jibrail is our enemy. He always comes to us with news of disaster, destruction and warning of troubles. Alas! If this enmity did not exist; we would have accepted Islam." The Prophet replied in the words of the Qur'an:

قُلْ مَن كَانَ عَدُوًّا لِجِبْرِيلَ فَإِنَّهُۥ نَزَّلَهُۥ عَلَىٰ قَلْبِكَ بِإِذْنِ ٱللَّهِ
مُصَدِّقًا لِّمَا بَيْنَ يَدَيْهِ وَهُدًى وَبُشْرَىٰ لِلْمُؤْمِنِينَ ۝

Say: "Whosoever is an enemy to Jibrail,
for indeed he has brought it (the Qur'an) down to your heart by Allah's
permission, confirming what came before it
(Torah and the Injeel) and guidance and glad tidings for the believers.

(Baqarah 2 : v 97)

They would also ridicule certain revelations; thus when the
following Ayah was revealed:

مَّن ذَا ٱلَّذِى يُقْرِضُ ٱللَّهَ قَرْضًا حَسَنًا فَيُضَٰعِفَهُۥ لَهُۥٓ أَضْعَافًا كَثِيرَةً

Who is he that will lend to Allah a goodly loan so that
He may multiply it to him many times?

(Baqarah 2 : v 245)

They began to ridicule that Allah had become such a pauper that
He was seeking loans from his servants. They would ask how the
Qur'an is the word of Allah when it mentions lowly insignificant
creatures such as flies and mosquitoes; the Qur'an again replies:

۞ إِنَّ ٱللَّهَ لَا يَسْتَحْىِۦٓ أَن يَضْرِبَ مَثَلًا مَّا بَعُوضَةً فَمَا
فَوْقَهَا فَأَمَّا ٱلَّذِينَ ءَامَنُوا فَيَعْلَمُونَ أَنَّهُ ٱلْحَقُّ مِن
رَّبِّهِمْ وَأَمَّا ٱلَّذِينَ كَفَرُوا فَيَقُولُونَ مَاذَآ أَرَادَ ٱللَّهُ
بِهَٰذَا مَثَلًا يُضِلُّ بِهِۦ كَثِيرًا وَيَهْدِى بِهِۦ كَثِيرًا
وَمَا يُضِلُّ بِهِۦٓ إِلَّا ٱلْفَٰسِقِينَ ۝

Verily Allah is not ashamed to set forth a parable of a mosquito or so much
more when it is bigger than it. And for those who believe, they know that it is
the truth from their Lord; as for those who disbelieve they say:
"What did Allah intend by this parable?"
By it He misleads many and many He guides thereby.

And misleads thereby only those who are the Fasiqoon (the rebellious).
(Baqarah 2 : v 26)

Emergence of Hypocrites

Alongside the growth of the Jewish opposition, a group of hypocrites began to be formed. The hypocrites outwardly had accepted Islam but had in fact hostile feelings against Islam. They worked among the Muslims aiming to gather information and exploit situations. Among the prominent men of the tribe of Banu Qaynuqa who were among this group were Zayd Ibn Lusayt, Riffa Ibn Zayd, Sa'd Ibn Hanifa, Nu`man Ibn Ufy, Kinana Ibn Surya and the leader of the hypocrites, Abdullah Ibn Ubayy. He had developed a great hatred for Prophet Muhammad; for it was the Prophet who had deprived him of the leadership of Madinah. On one occasion, whilst riding past Abdullah Ibn Ubayy, he greeted him, but Abdullah turned his face away. The Prophet recited some verses reminding him of the fear of Allah. Abdullah replied: "O Man! This manner of your talk is not suitable. Sit at home and talk to people who come to you. Do not bother those who do not come to you, for here this talk is not liked." The Prophet remained silent.

The movement of the hypocrites was to continue throughout the Madinan life. They continued to exploit the Muslims, create doubts, start false rumours and hold secret meetings planning to weaken the Islamic State.

The Obligation of Zakah

During this period, in the second year of Hijrah, Zakat was made

128

an obligation upon all the Muslims. It was an annual tax given by the Muslims, collected and then re-distributed by the State amongst the poor. The Qur'an outlines those entitled to Zakah:

إِنَّمَا ٱلصَّدَقَٰتُ لِلْفُقَرَآءِ وَٱلْمَسَٰكِينِ وَٱلْعَٰمِلِينَ عَلَيْهَا وَٱلْمُؤَلَّفَةِ قُلُوبُهُمْ وَفِى ٱلرِّقَابِ وَٱلْغَٰرِمِينَ وَفِى سَبِيلِ ٱللَّهِ وَٱبْنِ ٱلسَّبِيلِ فَرِيضَةً مِّنَ ٱللَّهِ وَٱللَّهُ عَلِيمٌ حَكِيمٌ

As Sadaqat (here it means Zakah) are only for:
1. Fuqara poor people who do not beg
2. Al Masakin, the poor who beg and
3. Those employed to collect the (funds) and to
4. Attract the hearts of those who have been inclined (towards Islam)
5. To free the captives and
6. For those in debt and
7. In the cause of Allah (Mujahideen) and for
8. The Wayfarer (a traveller who is cut off from everything);
A duty imposed by Allah. And Allah is All Knower, All Wise.
(Tawba 9 : v 60)

Fast of Ramadhan is Enjoined

At the same time with Zakah, fasting was enjoined for the Muslims in the month of Ramadhan. The Muslims had to abstain from food, drink and sexual relations from dawn to sunset. The Qur'an explains the purpose:

يَٰٓأَيُّهَا ٱلَّذِينَ ءَامَنُوا كُتِبَ عَلَيْكُمُ ٱلصِّيَامُ كَمَا كُتِبَ عَلَى ٱلَّذِينَ مِن قَبْلِكُمْ لَعَلَّكُمْ تَتَّقُونَ ۝

O you who believe! Fasting is prescribed for you as it was prescribed for those before you, so that you may become Al Muttaqeen (those who fear Allah).

(Al Baqarah 2 : v 183)

Fasting provided the Muslims with spiritual and physical training in their ultimate pursuit - to seek the pleasure of Allah.

Early Conditions of the Muslims

The material resources of Madinah were limited. When the Muhajirun from Makkah migrated to Madinah; they along with the Ansar had to face starvation because of the shortage of food. Although the Islamic State had been established, it was in its evolutionary and early stages; thus the immediate problems could not be solved instantly. Furthermore, the Quraish had declared economic sanctions against the people of Madinah. All tribes under the leadership of the Quraish, severed links with the city. The Muhajirun had to face a drastic change of diet. In Makkah they had been used to a diet of meat and milk whereas in Madinah dates constituted the major portion of their diet. Many were on the verge of death. Amir when sensing his death approaching said:

I have found death before tasting it and verily the death of a coward descends from above him.

Abu Bakr was also in a similar situation and used to say:

Every morning finds a man with a member of his family; But death is nearer to him than his shoe lace

On another occasion Abu Hurayra and Umar Ibn Al Khattab were discussing a verse of the Qur'an, when suddenly both became unconscious due to lack of food. When A'isha was asked: "Do you have a lantern?" Her reply illustrated the desperate situation in Madinah: "If we had oil to burn a lantern, we would have drunk it."

Public Treasury is Established

Prophet Muhammad established a public treasury *(Baitul Mal)* as a vital component of the economic system of the Islamic State. The Baitul Mal consisted of income from the limited resources of Madinah and donations *(Sadaqah)* by those who could afford it. The money from the Baitul Mal was distributed amongst the poor, those facing financial difficulties and those in debt. In-charge of the institution of Baitul Mal was Bilal.

The Jews planned to exploit the financial difficulties faced by the Muslims by demanding their loans to be paid back immediately. Jabir Ibn Abdullah had taken a loan from a Jew and could not pay it back in time because of the bad produce of dates that year. However, he obtained more time, but the harvest was also poor. This time the Jew demanded the repayment of the loan without any extensions. Jabir went to the Prophet and explained the situation. The Prophet then told Bilal to help Jabir repay the loan by taking out resources from the Baitul Mal.

JIHAD: STRUGGLE IN THE WAY OF ALLAH [1]

In Makkah the Quraish continued to persecute the Muslims who had remained, mainly consisting of women and slaves who had been unable to migrate. The houses and properties of the Muhajirun were burnt and destroyed, but the Muslims were told not to retaliate or defend their cause. However, the situation finally reached to such an extent that the following verses were revealed on the 11th of Safar in the second year of Hijrah:

Permission to fight is given to those who are being fought because they (believers) have been wronged and surely Allah is able to give them victory. Those who have been expelled from their homes unjustly only because they had said: "Our Lord is Allah."
(Al Hajj 22 : v 39-40)

Thus permission to fight the enemies of Allah had been given. For thirteen years the Muslims had tolerated the persecution of the Quraish; many witnessed the torture of their relatives and friends at the hands of the leaders of the Quraish. It was inappropriate to retaliate in Makkah, as the movement was in its evolutionary stage.

[1.] Jihad literally means exerting ones utmost. In the meaning of the Shari'ah it means to exert ones utmost in the path of Allah; this could take the form of purification of the souls, gaining knowledge, propagating the message of Islam etc. Put simply, Jihad refers to an all round struggle in order to lead a life as a Muslim. It is a pillar of Islam which protects and propagates Islam. The last stage of Jihad is Qital (the physical fighting i.e armies, weapons, war plan etc.). This can be offensive and defensive depending on the context. Evading the duty of Jihad in the form of Qital means the end to State. Opposing forces will come forward and dismantle the State and establish their rule. Thus the purpose of Qital is not to kill but to destroy or weaken the leadership of the enemy.

The period in Makkah had also been a training ground in which the qualities they acquired proved to be vital in later years (steadfastness, patience, political awareness, sacrifice, purity of intention etc.). Allah had also given them the permission to fight because in His sight:

وَصَدٌّ عَن سَبِيلِ ٱللَّهِ

وَكُفْرٌ بِهِۦ وَٱلْمَسْجِدِ ٱلْحَرَامِ وَإِخْرَاجُ أَهْلِهِۦ مِنْهُ أَكْبَرُ

عِندَ ٱللَّهِ وَٱلْفِتْنَةُ أَكْبَرُ مِنَ ٱلْقَتْلِ وَلَا يَزَالُونَ يُقَٰتِلُونَكُمْ

حَتَّىٰ يَرُدُّوكُمْ عَن دِينِكُمْ

But a greater (transgression) in the sight of Allah is to prevent mankind from following the way of Allah, to disbelieve in Him, to prevent access to Masjid al Haram and to drive out its inhabitants, and Al Fitnah (polytheism, persecution) is worse than killing. And they will never cease fighting you until they turn you back from your Deen.

(Baqarah 2 : v 217)

Events Leading up to Badr

The Quraish were longing to attack Madinah and destroy Islam. However, they first required an excuse to attack Madinah and secondly, gather support from other tribes. The means by which this was to be achieved, was to display their power and might in front of the other tribes. They believed that the free and unchecked movement of their caravans to Syria, passing by Madinah would show their might and thus the Muslims would be seen as weak in front of the rest of Arabia. Therefrom, many caravans were sent to Syria from Makkah.

Prophet Muhammad was aware of this strategy and had already

sent small parties with the intention of making the Makkans feel their presence. He had also ordered Ka'b Ibn Mailk to erect boundary pillars around Madinah. Some of the small parties guarded the frontiers of the State of Madinah and small skirmishes occurred.

Once, the Prophet marched with a party of one hundred and fifty (150) men to Zul Ushayra and returned after concluding pacts with Banu Damra and Banu Mudlij. However, during the patrol to Nakhda, under the leadership of Abdullah Ibn Jahsh, they clashed with a party of the Quraish and a few people were killed. The Prophet disliked what had taken place and compensated for those killed, as the objective of the parties was not confrontation.

Meanwhile, the Quraish had obtained support from Banu Kinana and concluded pacts with the tribes of Banu Nadir, Banu Laik and Banu Mutyib. The finance of the war was met by all of the people of Makkah.

The Prophet in Madinah received news that a caravan was passing very close to Madinah under the leadership of Abu Sufyan. The Prophet marched out with three hundred and thirteen (313) men, in order to intercept the caravan, which was in a position endangering the security of Madinah. Abu Sufyan on hearing the news led his caravan off the main route and travelled towards the Red Sea. He also sent an urgent summons to Makkah for reinforcements to protect the caravan, which he said was in danger of being captured by Prophet Muhammad and his companions.

The news of a Muslim army approaching the caravan of Abu Sufyan had reached Makkah. The messenger who was sent by Abu

Sufyan had exaggerated and gave the idea that the caravan had been ambushed. The Quraish gathered one thousand (1,000) soldiers of whom six hundred (600) were in armour, and seven hundred (700) camels and horses all under the leadership of Abu Jahl.

Preparations for War

News of the preparations made by the Quraish reached the Muslims. Prophet Muhammad held a shura (consultation meeting) with his companions, taking into account the gravity of the situation. The shura meeting took place at Zafran, a valley where the Muslim army had halted. Abu Bakr was the first to assure the Prophet of their unconditional obedience to his command. Umar was the next to support the view of Abu Bakr. Then Al Miqdad stood up and said: "O Messenger of Allah! Proceed whenever Allah directs you, for we are all with you. We will not say as the tribe of Bani Israil said to Musa 'Go you with your Lord and fight and we will stay here'; rather we shall say 'Go you with your Lord and fight and we will fight along with you.'

The Prophet was impressed by the determination and spirit of sacrifice for the sake of Islam and thus decided to confront the Makkan army; placing total reliance on Allah as they were ill equipped with an army of three hundred and thirteen (313) men of whom sixty (60) were from the Muhajirun and the rest were from the Ansar. They had seventy (70) camels and two (2) horses of which one belonged to Zubayr.

Abu Sufyan sent word to Abu Jahl that his caravan was in safety and that the Makkan army should return back to Makkah.

However, Abu Jahl insisted on continuing the march to eliminate the Muslims; he was not to let a chance like this pass by. Hakim Ibn Hazm and Utbah Ibn Rabiah also wanted to return, but Abu Jahl blocked any further defections.

The Muslims had taken a position facing the valley of Badr whilst the Quraish were on the other side of the valley. The Muslims dug a reservoir and filled it with water from the wells nearby and made a barrier around it. The Prophet spent the entire night preceding the day of the battle in prayer and supplication: "O Allah! Here are the Quraish exalted with pride and vanity and want to stop Your servants from worshipping You and to falsify Your Prophet. So send us Your promised help. O Allah! If this small number is routed today there will be none to worship You till the end of the days."

This was to be the most critical moment in the life of the movement as well as the Prophet. The outcome of this war would result in either the dominance or the extinction of Islam. Regardless of the fact that the Muslims were ill-equipped, they had strength of faith in their mission and had as their vision - Jannah.

The night before the battle, heavy rain fell. The Qur'an says:

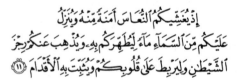

When He covered you with a slumber as a security from Him, and He caused water (rain) to descend on you from the sky, to clean you thereby and to remove from you the Rijz (evil suggestions) of Shaitan, and to strengthen your hearts, and make your feet firm thereby.

(Anfal 8 : v 11)

BATTLE OF BADR

On the morning of the 17th of Ramadhan, in the 2nd year of Hijrah, the Makkan and Muslim armies advanced and drew closer to one another. The rain which had fallen the previous night had been heavier on the side of the Quraish, making it difficult to move on the ground. As was the common procedure adopted in battles in Arabia, Utbah Ibn Rabiah, Shaybah Ibn Rabiah and Walid Ibn Utbah stepped out of line and insulted the Muslims and recited the achievement of their leaders. To oppose them, three youths came out from the Ansar: Awf Ibn Harith, Muawiyah Ibn Harith and Abdullah Ibn Rawdah; such was the bravery of the youth. However, the Quraish wanted older people who had migrated to Madinah. Upon this the Prophet told his uncle Hamza, Ubaydah Ibn Harith and Ali to go forward and face the opponents. The duels did not last long; all three from the Makkan army had been killed whilst Ubaydah was seriously wounded. As he lay awaiting death he asked the Prophet: "Am I not a Martyr *(Shaheed)* O Messenger of Allah?" The Prophet replied: "Indeed you are."

Whilst the Prophet, as the military head of the army, was organising the Muslim soldiers, a companion named Sawdah stepped out of line intentionally. The Prophet poked him in the side with an arrow, to which Sawdah expressed his pain. The Prophet lifted his own shirt and said: "Then do the same to me." Sawdah approached him and kissed him instead and said: "O Messenger of Allah! You know what is before us and I may not survive the battle. If this is my last time with you the last thing I want to do in this life is this."

Having examined the ranks, the Prophet proceeded to a shelter made of palm trees, from which he could command the battle. Abu Bakr, Sa'd Ibn Muadh and several others from the Ansar stood outside guarding the Prophet. Such was the inspiration and dynamism in the leadership of Prophet Muhammad that Umayr, a boy of sixteen, flung away some dates he was eating and cried out: "These are holding me back from Paradise," and plunged into the battle, later to die as a shaheed.

The battle commenced and the Quraish suffered great losses. Abu Jahl, the arch enemy of the Prophet was killed at the hands of two youths of the Ansar. However, the Muslims were not alone in their struggle against the Quraish; Allah had answered the Prophet's supplications and as the Qur'an explains:

When you sought help of Your Lord and He answered you:
"I will help you with a thousand of the angels each behind the other in succession." Allah made it only as glad tidings, and that your hearts be at rest therewith. And there is no victory except from Allah.
Verily, Allah is All Mighty, All Wise.
(Anfal 8 : v 9-10)

The angels were helping the Muslims combat the enemies of Allah and they had also received instructions from Allah:

إِذْ يُوحِى رَبُّكَ إِلَى ٱلْمَلَـٰٓئِكَةِ أَنِّى مَعَكُمْ فَثَبِّتُوا۟ ٱلَّذِينَ ءَامَنُوا۟ سَأُلْقِى فِى قُلُوبِ ٱلَّذِينَ كَفَرُوا۟ ٱلرُّعْبَ فَٱضْرِبُوا۟ فَوْقَ ٱلْأَعْنَاقِ وَٱضْرِبُوا۟ مِنْهُمْ كُلَّ بَنَانٍ ۝

When your Lord inspired the angels: "Verily I am with you, so keep firm those
who have believed. I will cast terror into the hearts of those who have
disbelieved, so strike them over their necks and smite over all their fingers and toes."

(Anfal 8 : v 12)

The presence of the angels was felt by all: as a strength by the
believers and as a terror by the disbelievers. However, the presence
was only audible or visible to a few. In one instance during the
battle, one of the believers was pursuing a man from the Quraish
and the man's head flew off before he could reach him; struck off
by an unseen hand. Others had brief glimpses of the angels led by
Jibrail. At another point in the battle, where the resistance of the
Quraish was at its strongest, a sword broke in the hands of a
believer and his first reaction was to go to the Prophet. The Prophet
gave him a wooden club saying : "Fight with this!" He took it and
brandished it, it became in his hand a long strong gleaming sword.
He fought with it for the rest of the Battle of Badr (and in other
battles to come and thus the sword was known as Al Awn - the
Divine help).

The Muslim army held its ground against the great might of the
Quraish and fought bravely, with determination and Paradise as
their reward. The ill-equipped Muslim army was creating fear in
the hearts of the Quraish. Umayyah Ibn Khalaf was killed by his
former slave Bilal, along with other leaders of the Quraish. Most of
them did not hesitate to retreat and some of them were captured by
the Muslims. The Prophet sent word to Madinah to tell the people

of the victory and then gathered the spoils of war in order to distribute them equally amongst the Muslims.

The Battle of Badr reminded the Muslims that real strength lies with faith in Allah and not in numbers and weapons. This Battle decided the course of the future history of the Muslims; who were now more determined after the victory. The Qur'an says:

فَلَمْ تَقْتُلُوهُمْ وَلَكِنَّ ٱللَّهَ قَتَلَهُمْ

You killed them not, but Allah killed them.
(Anfal 8 : v 17)

Prisoners of War

The outcome of the Battle of Badr resulted in the loss of twenty two (22) Muslim Soldiers, seventy (70) men were killed from the Quraish and another seventy two (72) captured by the Muslims. Most of the leaders - Abu Jahl, Umayyah Ibn Khalaf; Abul Bhukhtari and Zamlah Ibn Aswad had been killed. The strength of the Makkans had been shattered and they had been humiliated in the sight of Arabia.

From among the seventy two prisoners of war, two were executed: Uqabah Ibn Abi Muayat and Al Nadir Ibn al Harith. They were known for their deep hostility towards Islam. The fate of the remaining prisoners lay awaiting. Several opinions were put forward: Sa'd Ibn Muadh suggested: "This is the first defeat Allah has inflicted on the idolaters and I would rather see their men slaughtered than allowed to live." Umar Ibn al Khattab was also of the same opinion. However, Abu Bakr was in favour of releasing the prisoners with a ransom, in the hope that sooner or later they would accept Islam and the Prophet inclined to this view. Later on that day, Umar returned to the shelter to find the Prophet and Abu Bakr in tears on account of the following verses:

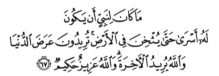

It is not for a Prophet that he should have prisoners of war
(and free them with ransom) until he had made a great slaughter (among his enemies) in the land. You desire the good of this world, but Allah desires (for you) the good of the Hereafter. And Allah is All Mighty, All Wise.
(Anfal 8 :v 67)

Allah had affirmed the opinion of Umar Ibn al Khattab but later revelation made it clear that the decision to spare the captives had been accepted by Allah. The Prophet was given a message from Allah to deliver to the prisoners of war:

يَٰٓأَيُّهَا ٱلنَّبِيُّ قُل لِّمَن فِىٓ أَيۡدِيكُم مِّنَ ٱلۡأَسۡرَىٰٓ إِن يَعۡلَمِ ٱللَّهُ
فِى قُلُوبِكُمۡ خَيۡرٗا يُؤۡتِكُمۡ خَيۡرٗا مِّمَّآ أُخِذَ مِنكُمۡ وَيَغۡفِرۡ لَكُمۡۗ
وَٱللَّهُ غَفُورٞ رَّحِيمٞ ۝

O Prophet! Say to the captives that are in your hands: "If Allah knows any good in your hearts, He will give you something better than what has been taken from you. And He will forgive you and Allah is Oft-Forgiving, Most Merciful.
(Anfal 8 : v 70)

Abu Jahl's body was searched for by Abdullah Ibn Masud in order to confirm his death. He found Abu Jahl, who still had enough life in him to recognise Abdullah. Abdullah had been the first man to recite the Qur'an aloud in front of the Ka'bah and it was Abu Jahl who struck him and wounded his face. Abdullah placed his foot on the neck of Abu Jahl, who uttered: "You have climbed high little shepherd." Abdullah simply replied: "Allah and His Messenger have won today," and cut off his head.

The Prophet gave orders that the prisoners of war be treated kindly and with justice. One of the prisoners later said: "Blessings on the men of Madinah; they gave us wheaten bread to eat when there was little of it and contenting themselves with dates." Many of the captives had experienced for the first time the beauty of Islam and became Muslims. Others were released on ransom ranging from one thousand to four thousand dirhams. The poor were set free without any ransom.

The prisoners who could read and write were each entrusted with ten children with the condition that they would be released once the children were capable of reading and writing. There is no better example than this, illustrating the value Islam attached to education. Knowledge and Islam became two inseperable entities in the lives of the companions.

In-between Badr and Uhud

Although the Muslims had been victorious at the Battle of Badr, the Qur'an reminded them that their struggle had to continue until the aim was fulfilled:

وَقَٰتِلُوهُمْ حَتَّىٰ لَا تَكُونَ فِتْنَةٌ وَيَكُونَ ٱلدِّينُ كُلُّهُ لِلَّهِ

And fight them until there is no more fitnah (injustice, worshipping others besides Allah) and the deen (worship) will be all for Allah alone.

(Anfal 8 : v 39)

Seeking revenge was the only thought of every Quraish in Makkah, especially Abu Sufyan and his wife Hind. The latter had lost her father and brother at Badr. Furthermore, in order to retain their power and prestige in Arabia it was essential that they defeat the Muslims in another battle.

Leading up to the Battle of Uhud, small skirmishes had occurred between the believers and disbelievers. The tribe of Banu Qaynuqa had been besieged by the Muslims for violating its pledge and supporting the Quraish at Badr. Two months after the Battle of Badr, Abu Sufyan came to Madinah with two hundred men and tried to attack the city in co-operation with Salma Ibn Miskham, but was unsuccessful and made a retreat. The Prophet went in pursuit but Abu Sufyan had escaped, leaving bags of dried powder in order to lighten their burden. The bags proved useful for the Muslims and therefrom the incident was known as Ghazwa Sawiq (expedition of dried flour).

The Quraish started a full scale preparation for revenge. Envoys were sent to different tribes to secure support and build up hatred against the Muslims. Eventually a large army of three thousand (3000) soldiers; seven hundred (700) of whom were in armour marched towards the valley of Uhud and encamped at Uhud. Even the prominent women of Makkah - Hind, Umm Hakim, Raithah, Barsa and others came to support the Makkan army. Everyone who lived in Makkah had contributed to the cost of the preparations of the Makkan army. The Qur'an in reference to this says:

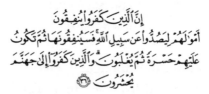

Verily those who disbelieve spend their wealth to hinder (men) from the Path of Allah, and so will they continue to spend it; but in the end it will become an anguish for them. Then they will be overcome. And those who disbelieve will be gathered into Hell.

(Anfal 8 : v 36)

An Abyssinian slave named Wahshi also joined the army and was known for his accuracy with a spear. Jubayr Ibn al Mutim, his master had agreed with him that if he kills Hamza, the Uncle of the Prophet Muhammad, he would be set free. Hind had also told him that if he carries out Jubayr's order she will clothe him in gold and silver.

News reached Madinah on the 5th of Shawwal (3rd year of Hijrah) of a new Makkan army. The Prophet gathered the elders and youth of Madinah in a Shura meeting to discuss the arrangements to be made. The Majority of the Muhajirun and the elders of Ansar suggested that they should stay in the city of Madinah and defend from within. However the youth, who were more determined and courageous, proposed to combat the Quraish outside Madinah. The Prophet accepted the proposal given by the youth and put on his armour. The enthusiasm of the youth to participate in the Jihad made some stand on their toes to increase their heights (for they were too small i.e. 12 -13 years of age) so as not to be recognised by the Prophet. Some of the women of Madinah including A'isha, Umm Sulaym and Umm Saulayt accompanied the Muslim army.

After the Friday Prayers, the Prophet marched out with one thousand (1000) men, including Abdullah Ibn Ubayy, the leader of the hypocrites. However, he deserted at Shuth with three hundred (300) of his followers. He had wanted to stay in Madinah and fight and since he was a hypocrite he did not want to lose his life in the cause of Allah and Islam. Hence, the Muslim army was reduced to seven hundred (700) soldiers and two hundred (200) horses and was to face an army of three thousand (3000) soldiers.

BATTLE OF UHUD

When the Muslim army reached the Mount of Uhud, Prophet Muhammad started positioning his soldiers. He placed fifty archers under the command of Abdullah Ibn Jubayr, on top of the mountain and told them not to leave their positions under any circumstances. Hamza was to command the infantry and Zubayr Ibn Awwam was given the command of the cavalry.

After they had been positioned, the Prophet held up his sword and said: "Who will use this sword with its rights?" Many asked for the honour, but it was given to Abu Dujanah.

Abu Amir, from the side of the Quraish was the first to open the battle but had to return to his line because of a shower of stones thrown at him by the Muslims. Again the duels took place and the three Muslim soldiers succeeded in killing three enemies of Islam. During the battle, the Quraish suffered heavy losses and dismay began to be spread in the Makkan camp.

As the battle continued, a group of fourteen Makkan women began to encourage the Makkan soldiers, singing:

> We are the daughters of stars; and walk on carpets,
> If you advance, we hug you; if you retreat we leave you.

Abu Dujanah, was displaying wonderful skills of fighting and even in the midst of the battle was aware of his responsibility. He later said: "During the battle I saw someone urging the enemy; I went to kill that person and when I lifted my sword above the person's head, the person screamed. I realised it was a woman and obeyed the Prophet's order of not killing women and children and left her. I later found out it was Hind."

Victory then Defeat

The Muslims were finding themselves to be victorious as the Quraish were in a state of confusion and intending to retreat. The following Ayah indicates that the Muslims were gaining the upper hand with the permission of Allah:

$$وَلَقَدْ صَدَقَكُمُ ٱللَّهُ وَعْدَهُۥ إِذْ تَحُسُّونَهُم بِإِذْنِهِۦ$$

And Allah did fulfil His promise to you when you were killing them (your enemy) with His Permission.
(Al Imran 3 : v 152)

When the Muslim archer's saw that the Quraish were retreating they said to Abdullah Ibn Jubayr: "The booty! The booty! Our companions have won, so what are you waiting for?" Abdullah answered: "Have you forgotten what the Messenger of Allah said to you?" However they replied: "By God, we are going to join the people and take our share of the booty." So forty of the fifty archers ran down the mountain onto the battlefield.

Khalid Ibn Walid, commander of the Quraish cavalry saw the opportunity for a counter attack. From the back of the mountain he attacked Abdullah Ibn Jubayr and the remaining archers and defeated them. He then proceeded with his cavalry to attack the Muslims from behind. The Muslims had lost their position and began to fight without any organisation or plan. Many of the

Muslims had fled the battlefield. It was during this disorder that Hamza the uncle of Prophet Muhammad was killed by Wahshi. The Quraish seeing this golden opportunity returned from retreating and started to attack the Muslims; thus now gaining the upper hand.

A rumour began to be spread that the Prophet had been killed. The reactions of the Muslim soldiers were different. Some saw it of no use to continue fighting without the Prophet and thus fled towards the mountains. To them, victory was nothing without the Prophet.

Others saw it of no use to live without the Prophet and continued fighting, hoping to obtain martyrdom. Anas Ibn al Nadar was one such person. When he heard the Prophet had died, he faced his opponent, Sa'd Ibn Muadh, and said: "O Sa'd! By the Lord of An Nadr; Paradise! I am smelling the scent of Paradise coming from the Mountain of Uhud." Later, when his body was discovered, more than eighty wounds and arrows were found on his body. It was mutilated so badly that none except his sister could recognise him and identified him by his fingers. The Qur'an describes such people:

$$\text{مِنَ ٱلْمُؤْمِنِينَ رِجَالٌ صَدَقُوا مَا عَـٰهَدُوا ٱللَّهَ عَلَيْـهِ}$$

Among the believers are men who have been true to their covenant with Allah (i.e. they have gone out for Jihad) and showed not their backs (to the disbelievers).
(Ahzab 33 : v 23)

Ka'b Ibn Malik found that the Prophet was alive and informed the Muslims. The Prophet had shown no sign of anxiety or weakness, his feet neither staggered nor wavered at this critical situation. He himself had been attacked, but was defended by Abu Talha, Sa'd Ibn Abu Waqqas and five other Muslim soldiers. Nevertheless his tooth was broken and he received a wound on his face. As blood was flowing from his face he wiped it saying: "How can a people prosper who have bloodied the face of their Prophet whilst he is calling them to Islam." Allah reminded him:

$$\text{لَيْسَ لَكَ مِنَ ٱلْأَمْرِ شَيْءٌ أَوْ يَتُوبَ عَلَيْهِمْ أَوْ يُعَذِّبَهُمْ فَإِنَّهُمْ ظَالِمُونَ ﴿١٢٨﴾}$$

Not for you is the decision whether He turns in mercy to (pardons) them or punishes them; verily they are the wrong doers.
(Imran 3 :v 128)

The Prophet prayed to Allah: "O My Lord! Forgive and guide my people for they know not." Whilst the Muslims were retreating from the battlefield, following the defeat, Abu Sufyan called out: "Victory for war goes by turns; today in exchange for Badr." The Prophet heard this and told Umar to answer Abu Sufyan saying:

"Allah is the Most High and Most Gracious. We are not equal for our dead are in Paradise and your dead in Hell."

Quraish Mutilate the Dead

The Quraish were extremely happy and clamorous in their triumph over the Muslims at Uhud. They buried their dead, twenty two in total, then the women of Quraish, led by Hind, began to mutilate the martyred Muslims on the battlefield. The black slave Wahshi, who was hired to kill Hamza in return for his freedom, showed Hind the dead body of Hamza. Hind immediately ordered the body to be cut open. She then took out his liver and chewed it. She

149

is even reported to have made a necklace out of the liver.

The Muslims returned to the battlefield after the Quraish had left. Prophet Muhammad, on seeing his uncle Hamza lying dead and mutilated, was deeply saddened. He was furious to see Hamza in such a state. He took off his own cloak and wrapped it around Hamza and said: "There will never be a moment as sad for me as this. If ever Allah gives me victory over them, I shall mutilate them as the Arabs have never done before!" On this occasion the verse addresses the Prophet, saying:

وَإِنْ عَاقَبْتُمْ فَعَاقِبُوا بِمِثْلِ مَا عُوقِبْتُم بِهِ وَلَئِن صَبَرْتُمْ لَهُوَ خَيْرٌ لِّلصَّابِرِينَ ۝ وَاصْبِرْ وَمَا صَبْرُكَ إِلَّا بِاللَّهِ وَلَا تَحْزَنْ عَلَيْهِمْ وَلَا تَكُ فِي ضَيْقٍ مِّمَّا يَمْكُرُونَ ۝ إِنَّ اللَّهَ مَعَ الَّذِينَ اتَّقَوا وَّالَّذِينَ هُم مُّحْسِنُونَ ۝

And if you punish (your enemy), then punish them the like of that with which you were inflicted. But if you endure patiently, verily, it is better for the patient. And endure you patiently, your patience is not but from Allah. And grieve not over them, and be not distressed because of what they plot. Truly, Allah is with those who fear Him, (keep their duty to Him), and those who are Muhsinun (doers of good).
(An Nahl 16 : v 126-128)

On hearing these verses, Prophet Muhammad decided to forgive the Quraish and also forbade the Muslims to mutilate dead bodies.

After the Battle

After this event, the Prophet and the Muslim army marched in the direction of Makkah to pursue the Quraish and to show that the

Muslims were still able to fight. They followed the Quraish up to a distance of eight miles and stopped at a place named Hamra Al Asad. The Quraish had in fact at this moment halted and had planned to attack Madinah, but learning of the Muslim army's approach, they feared that the Muslims had brought reinforcements from Madinah. Abu Sufyan decided to send one of his companions to spy on the Muslims camped at Hamra Al Asad. The companion returned and reported that he had never seen such numbers or such readiness, all burning to fight the Quraish. Upon hearing this news, Abu Sufyan and his army had no courage to fight the determined Muslims and thus decided to return to Makkah. Prophet Muhammad and the Muslims remained at Hamra Al Asad for five days and after being completely satisfied that the Makkan army had departed, they returned to Madinah. (It is for this reason some historians state that the Battle of Uhud was a draw and not a defeat for the Muslims).

On returning to Madinah, the Prophet swore that no Muslim who had died a martyr would want to come back to life for a single hour even if he could own the whole world; unless he could return and fight for Allah and be killed a second time.

Disobedience to the Prophet and the desire for materialistic things were the two main reasons for the defeat of the Muslims at Uhud. Allah tested the Muslims at this battle, but they had failed. Nevertheless, since Allah is Merciful and Forgiving, Allah forgave the Muslims for their disobedient act:

وَلَقَدْ صَدَقَكُمُ اللَّهُ

وَعْدَهُۥٓ إِذْ تَحُسُّونَهُم بِإِذْنِهِۦ حَتَّىٰٓ إِذَا فَشِلْتُمْ

وَتَنَٰزَعْتُمْ فِى ٱلْأَمْرِ وَعَصَيْتُم مِّنۢ بَعْدِ مَآ أَرَىٰكُم

مَّا تُحِبُّونَ مِنكُم مَّن يُرِيدُ ٱلدُّنْيَا وَمِنكُم

مَّن يُرِيدُ ٱلْأَخِرَةَ ثُمَّ صَرَفَكُمْ عَنْهُمْ لِيَبْتَلِيَكُمْ

وَلَقَدْ عَفَا عَنكُمْ وَٱللَّهُ ذُو فَضْلٍ عَلَى ٱلْمُؤْمِنِينَ

And Allah did indeed fulfil His promise to you when you were killing therein
with His Permission; until you lost your courage and fell to disputing about
the order, and disobeyed after He showed you (of the booty) which you love.
Among you are some that desire this world and some that desire the Hereafter.
Then He made you flee from them (your enemy), that He might test you. But
surely, He forgave you, and Allah is Most Gracious to the believers. Then He
turned you from them, that He might try you and He has forgiven you and
Allah is bounteous to the believers.

(Al Imran 3: v 152)

Banu Asad Plan to Attack Madinah

In-spite of the courage shown by the Muslims when pursuing the
Quraish, some of the Arab tribes who resented the Prophet's
presence in Madinah thought that this was the ideal moment to
attack the Muslims (i.e. after their defeat at Uhud). Approximately
two months after Uhud, news reached Madinah that a certain tribe
named Banu Asad were coming to attack Madinah. The Prophet
immediately prepared an army of one hundred and fifty (150)
Muslims and put Abu Salma in charge. He ordered them to
travel by night and hide by day and take an uncommon route so
they may surprise their enemy which was far bigger and stronger.

In the fog of an early morning, the Muslims attacked the tribe of

Banu Asad, who in complete surprise could not defend nor attack. Abu Salma and the army of one hundred and fifty Muslims defeated the enemy. Abu Salma did not live long after this; as he was suffering from a re-opened wound.

The Three Martyrs

One day, a few people from two small tribes came to the Prophet saying that they wanted to enter Islam and needed teachers to guide and instruct them. The Prophet sent six of his companions with them, for his aim was to spread the message of Islam as far as he could.

The six companions and the people from the small tribes were passing through the land of Hudhayl when suddenly they found themselves being attacked by an army of a hundred people. Three of them died fighting and the remaining three were taken captives.

The attackers then decided to sell the remaining Muslims to the Quraish. On the way to Makkah one of the captives made an attempt to escape, the tribesmen could not catch up to him, so they exposed their brutal nature by stoning him to death. The other two were sold to the Quraish who were lusting for revenge.

One of the two captives was a man named Zayd. When he was about to be killed, Abu Sufyan asked him: "Zayd, would you not prefer to have Muhammad in your place being crucified and you safe with your family?" "No by Allah," answered Zayd, "I would not like a thorn to prick Muhammad's finger in exchange for my life and safety."

It was from such incidents that Abu Sufyan used to say: "I have never seen a man whose followers love him as the followers of Muhammad."

The other captive was Khubayb. He was imprisoned before he was to be killed. The woman at whose house he was imprisoned, sometimes forgot that he was the enemy because of the goodness of his character. When he was to be executed, he asked permission to pray. He prayed two rakats and would have prayed more but feared that the Quraish would think that he was praying in fear of death.

These two men died as martyrs **(Shuhada)**. They could have saved themselves by just rejecting Islam and returning to idol worship. But their faith **(Iman)** was so strong that they remained Muslims even when their lives were at stake. They could have verbally rejected Islam, as this is permitted in cases of life and death, but did not. The Qur'an says of such men:

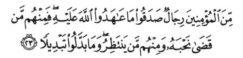

Among the Believers are men who have been true to their covenant with Allah.
Of them some have fulfilled their obligations, and some of them are still
waiting, but they have never changed in the least.
(Al Ahzab 33 :v 23)

This type of incident was not the last in its type. Many other Muslims were taken in a similar manner and killed. Behind all these brutal killings were the Quraish. On another occasion the Prophet Muhammad sent seventy (70) teachers to a tribe. On reaching a certain place they were killed by a large army, although one of them managed to escape. Such merciless butchering of innocent Muslim preachers by the Arab tribes was indeed very painful for the Prophet to bear, but it did not prevent the message of Islam from spreading further and further.

Banu Nadir's Plot to Kill The Prophet

During the next few years, the Jewish tribes who resented the Prophet's presence, began to cause trouble. They tried to create misunderstandings between Muslims and between the Muhajirun and the Ansar.

One of the Jewish tribes who were in the forefront of this campaign against the Muslims was a tribe named Banu Nadir. They were also one of the three tribes who signed the peace agreement with the Prophet Muhammad. They spied on the Muslims and informed the Quraish of their movements. They began to conspire and construct plots to kill the Prophet.

An opportunity to kill the Prophet was presented to them when Prophet Muhammad went with Abu Bakr, Umar and a few other companions to the tribe of Banu Nadir to discuss with them the compensation money that had to be paid for the two men of Banu Amir who had been killed by mistake.

They gave the Prophet a warm welcome and expressed their delight at his presence. In the meantime a plan was already formulated to throw a large rock from above while the Prophet sat discussing with the people of Banu Nadir. The son of Jash Ibn Ka'b, a Jew, was given the job to carry out the plot.

The Prophet sat with the leaders of Banu Nadir and was discussing the matter when suddenly he got up without saying anything and left. Everyone thought that he would come back and thus waited for him. Abu Bakr, Umar and the other companions having waited long enough, decided to leave and look for the Prophet. They found him in the mosque. The Prophet explained to them the evil plot of Banu Nadir to kill him. He then sent Muhammad Ibn Maslamah to Banu Nadir to inform them that they had broken the treaty by planning to kill him and that they had ten days to leave the city of Madinah. Anybody found after ten days would be killed.

Banu Nadir were shocked to find out that the Prophet knew their plan, even to the minutest detail. They said to Maslamah, who had been their ally before accepting Islam: "O Son of Maslamah! We never thought that it would be you who would bring such a message." "Hearts have changed," replied Ibn Maslamah.

Most of the people of Banu Nadir made preparations to leave the city, but Abdullah Ibn Ubayy Ibn Salul, the chief of the hypocrites, sent a message to them saying that he had an army of two thousand (2,000) people, who would defend them if the Muslims attacked. Inspired by this news, the people of Banu Nadir decided to stay and fight against the Muslims.

The ten days had expired and there was no sign of the army that Abdullah Ibn Ubayy had promised. Referring to this incident the Qur'an says:

أَلَمۡ تَرَ إِلَى

ٱلَّذِينَ نَافَقُواْ يَقُولُونَ لِإِخۡوَٰنِهِمُ ٱلَّذِينَ كَفَرُواْ مِنۡ أَهۡلِ ٱلۡكِتَٰبِ لَئِنۡ أُخۡرِجۡتُمۡ لَنَخۡرُجَنَّ مَعَكُمۡ وَلَا نُطِيعُ فِيكُمۡ أَحَدًا أَبَدًا وَإِن قُوتِلۡتُمۡ لَنَنصُرَنَّكُمۡ وَٱللَّهُ يَشۡهَدُ إِنَّهُمۡ لَكَٰذِبُونَ ⑪ لَئِنۡ أُخۡرِجُواْ لَا يَخۡرُجُونَ مَعَهُمۡ وَلَئِن قُوتِلُواْ لَا يَنصُرُونَهُمۡ وَلَئِن نَّصَرُوهُمۡ لَيُوَلُّنَّ ٱلۡأَدۡبَٰرَ ثُمَّ لَا يُنصَرُونَ ⑫

Have you not observed the hypocrites who say to their friends among the people of the Scripture who disbelieve: "If you are expelled we indeed will go out with you, and we shall never obey anyone against you, and if you are attacked, we shall indeed help you." But Allah is Witness, that they verily, are liars. Surely, if they (the Jews) are expelled, never will they (hypocrites) go out with them, and if they are attacked, they will never help them. And if they do help them, they will turn their backs, so they will not be victorious.

(Al Hashr 59 : v 11-12)

Banu Nadir were then attacked by the Muslims, since they had failed to comply with the ten day deadline. They were easily besieged by the Muslim army. They tried to gain the help of Banu Qurayzah, another Jewish tribe, but the latter refused saying that they did not wish to break the treaty with the Muslims. Banu Nadir waited for help for six days and eventually surrendered after realising that they had no other choice.

One of the leaders of Banu Nadir, a man named Huyay, sent a message saying that they would leave the city immediately. Prophet Muhammad accepted the plea as well as granting each of them the permission to take a camel's load of whatever they desired to carry with them. However, their lands and armour had to be given to the Prophet. Some of them travelled to Khaybar whilst others travelled to Azriat.

The land of Banu Nadir and all that was left behind was distributed by the Prophet to the poor and needy and especially to the poor emigrants who have been driven from their homes. Two of the Ansars received a share on account of their poverty. By giving most of the land to the Muhajirun, the Prophet made them independent of the Ansar of whom the Qur'an says:

وَٱلَّذِينَ تَبَوَّءُو ٱلدَّارَ وَٱلْإِيمَٰنَ مِن قَبْلِهِمْ
يُحِبُّونَ مَنْ هَاجَرَ إِلَيْهِمْ وَلَا يَجِدُونَ فِى صُدُورِهِمْ حَاجَةً
مِّمَّآ أُوتُواْ وَيُؤْثِرُونَ عَلَىٰٓ أَنفُسِهِمْ وَلَوْ كَانَ بِهِمْ خَصَاصَةٌ
وَمَن يُوقَ شُحَّ نَفْسِهِۦ فَأُوْلَٰٓئِكَ هُمُ ٱلْمُفْلِحُونَ ٩

And those who, before them, had homes and had adopted the Faith, love
those who emigrate to them, and have no jealousy in their breasts for that
which they have been given, and give them (emigrants) preference over
themselves, even though they were in need of that. And whosoever is saved
from his own covetousness, such are they who will be the successful.
(Al Hashr 59 :v 9)

The Second Badr

Abu Sufyan, after the battle of Uhud had challenged the Muslims to meet his army at Badr in a years time in order to decide which army had the upper hand since both the armies had lost one and won one. When the time drew near, the Prophet led an army of one thousand and five hundred (1500) men, the largest he had led so far, towards Badr.

Meanwhile, Abu Sufyan and the Quraish were faced with a problem: they did not have enough pasture to feed the animals if they travelled to Badr. Abu Sufyan thought that if the Quraish did not go to fight the Muslims at Badr, then it would be a shameful and dishonourable act for him since he was the one who proposed to meet the Muslims at Badr for a second time. He decided that if only he could stop the Muslims from coming to Badr then he would be able to claim that the Muslims broke the agreement. He sent Nu'aym, one of the leading men of Banu Ashja, to Madinah with the task of persuading the Muslims not to march to Badr.

Nu'aym went to Madinah and spoke to all sections of the community: the Ansar, the Muhajirun, the Jews and the Hypocrites *(Munafiqun)*. He tried to frighten the Muslims by saying: "Stay here and do not go against them. By God, I do not think a single one of you will escape with his life." He tried many more cunning tactics but not one succeeded.

The mission of Nu'aym had undoubtedly failed. He had failed to persuade the Muslims to stay at Madinah. Upon seeing this kind of attitude and commitment he was very impressed and realised the true meaning of Islam and thus became a Muslim. (This incident is just one of many examples supporting the Qur'anic statement: 'Whomsoever Allah wishes to guide, none can misguide.')

Upon hearing the news (the news did not include the fact that Nu'aym had become a Muslim) that the Muslims were marching towards Badr, Abu Sufyan decided that he would lead an army of two thousand (2,000) men towards Badr. After travelling for two days they would return to Makkah and claim that the Prophet and his army were nowhere to be seen at Badr.

He carried out this plan not knowing that the Prophet and the

Muslim army had waited eight days for the Quraish at Badr, during which the Muslims were able to trade and make profit, for Badr was a market place.

All the tribes over Arabia soon heard of the news that the Quraish had broken their word and that the Prophet had kept his. This was a moral and psychological victory for the Muslims. The Qur'an says:

ٱلَّذِينَ قَالَ لَهُمُ ٱلنَّاسُ إِنَّ ٱلنَّاسَ قَدْ جَمَعُوا۟ لَكُمْ فَٱخْشَوْهُمْ فَزَادَهُمْ إِيمَٰنًا وَقَالُوا۟ حَسْبُنَا ٱللَّهُ وَنِعْمَ ٱلْوَكِيلُ ۝ فَٱنقَلَبُوا۟ بِنِعْمَةٍ مِّنَ ٱللَّهِ وَفَضْلٍ لَّمْ يَمْسَسْهُمْ سُوٓءٌ وَٱتَّبَعُوا۟ رِضْوَٰنَ ٱللَّهِ وَٱللَّهُ ذُو فَضْلٍ عَظِيمٍ ۝

Those to whom men said:
"Verily the people have gathered against you, so fear them."
But this only increased them in faith and they said:
"Allah (alone) is Sufficient for us, and
He is the Best Disposer of affairs.
So they returned with grace and bounty from Allah.
No harm ever touched them, for they followed
the good pleasure of Allah and Allah
is the Owner of Great Bounty.
(Al Imran 3: v 173-174)

Even though the Arabian tribes could see clearly that the Muslims had become a formidable power, they did not come to terms with it. Instead many of these tribes would declare war on the Muslims. Whenever the Prophet heard of preparations for war by these tribes, he would send out an army to meet them, before they could march upon Madinah. In most incidents the tribes retreated.

BATTLE OF THE TRENCH

Jews Conspire with the Quraish

The Jews knew that they could not defeat the Muslims themselves, thus Huyay, the chief of the exiled Banu Nadir with some other leaders of other exiled tribes, went secretly to Makkah. The purpose of their trip was to enlist the help of the Quraish, who themselves were planning a final attack on Madinah to destroy Islam once and for all.

Intense secret planning and preparations began between the Jews and the Quraish. The latter enquired about Banu Qurayza, the only Jewish tribe not to have broken the treaty with the Prophet and the Muslims. Huyay Ibn Akhtab assured them that Banu Qurayza would also help and were actually waiting for the Quraish to attack Madinah. To convince, inspire and encourage the Quraish even more, they said that the religion of the Quraish (idol worship), was far better than the worship of Allah alone. This statement was in reply to the question posed by Abu Sufyan: "Is our religion better than theirs?" Concerning the reply given by the Jews, the Qur'an says:

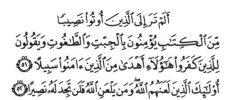

Have you not turned your thought to those who were
given a portion of the Book? They believe in sorcery and Tagut and say to the
disbelievers that they are better guided in the (right) way than the believers.

They are (men) whom Allah has cursed. And those whom Allah has cursed,
you will find, have no-one to help.

(An Nisa 4 : v 51-52)

The Jews then told the Quraish that if all the Arab tribes formed an army and attacked Madinah, the Jews inside the city would help in defeating the Muslims. They did not leave Makkah until they made the Quraish promise to fight the Muslims. The Jews then went to seven other tribes and promised them a clean victory and a share of the spoils.

A formidable army was gathered and Abu Sufyan was put in charge. The Quraish had four thousand (4,000) warriors, three hundred (300) horsemen and one thousand and five hundred (1500) men on war camels. A tribe named Banu Farcur came with thousands of warriors including one thousand (1,000) camel men. Other tribes had four hundred (400) or so warriors each, and Banu Asad also joined the army. In total there was an army of ten thousand (10,000) soldiers mobilised to attack Madinah (5th year of Hijrah).

Digging the Trench

Eventually the Muslims learnt of the preparations of the Jews and the Quraish to attack Madinah. The betrayal of the Jews did not surprise the Prophet Muhammad, who said of them: "The hearts of the Jews have become closed to the truth. They have forgotten what Musa taught them long ago that there is only One God."

Defending Madinah was now the main task for Prophet Muhammad and the Muslims. The Muslims decided to defend from within the city. On one side, the city had a natural defence of the town. On the other side, it was protected by the stone walls of houses, but there still remained one side open to attack. How were they to defend it?

Amongst the Muslims was a Persian named Salman, who had travelled to seek the truth and had found it in Islam. He had knowledge of war tactics that the Arabs had never heard of. His suggestion was that they should dig a trench around the exposed part of the city. The Muslims immediately started digging as they only had a week left before their enemies reached Madinah. All the Muslims joined in as they had done in the building of the mosque of the Prophet. All around there were the sounds of spades and pickaxes, and the shouts of the workers. The Prophet, while he worked with the Muslims again, sang:

"O Lord there is no happiness but in Paradise
Then have mercy on the Ansar and the Muhajirun."

The other workers who were covered with earth and dust answered:

"Unto Muhammad have we pledged our faith.
To fight his foes and flee not until his death."

Once when Prophet Muhammad was striking a large rock with his pickaxe, there was a great flash of light. He struck the rock again and there was another flash of light. This happened three times. Salman and the other companions asked him about the significance of this. He told them: "In the first flash of light, I saw the castles of Kisra. In the second flash of light, I saw the castles of Persia and in the third flash, I saw the castles of Byzantium."

This was a vision implying that one day the light of Islam would shine on these lands, who were at that time the major powers of the world. It was a vision to which the Muslims could look forward to even though they were in a vulnerable situation.

Hearing the reply given by the Prophet Muhammad, the Jews and hypocrites laughed and made fun of the Muslims. They would say: "The Muslims are about to be wiped off the face of earth and Muhammad tells them that the lands of Caesar and Chosroes will be theirs, and the fools believe him."

Yet, less than three years after the Prophet's death, these prophetic words were no longer a 'joke' but a historical fact. The Qur'an says:

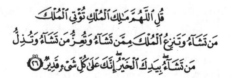

Say: "O Allah! Lord of power (and rule), You give power to whom You please, and You seize power from whom You please. You give honour to whom You please, and You bring low whom You please. In Your Hand is all good, verily over all things You have power."

(Al Imran 3 :v 26)

During the digging of the trench there was hardly any food available and the Muslims often worked in a state of hunger. However, on one occasion a bunch of dates was given to the Prophet Muhammad by a girl and the Prophet laid this out on a piece of cloth. Every worker was called to have a share of the dates which kept increasing in number until there were more dates than the cloth could hold.

The work continued. In six days, a fifteen foot (15ft) wide and five foot (5ft) deep trench had been dug along all the unprotected parts of the city. The houses outside the trench were vacated and all the women and children were placed in towers within the city. The preparations were barely finished when the Muslims saw a large force of ten thousand soldiers approaching the gates of Madinah.

The enemies of Islam were astonished and baffled at the new form of defence that had been set up by the Muslims. They had never seen such a thing in Arabia. Their initial plan was to attack Madinah, kill the Muslims, loot the goods and return to Makkah victorious. But now this was not possible. They could not get across to attack Madinah. The Muslims always pushed them back. In their desperation they decided to set up a camp with the intention of starving the Muslims into surrender.

Banu Qurayza are Persuaded

The ten thousand soldiers began to get rather restless during this long wait. Huyay Ibn Akhtat, the chief of Banu Nadir feared that some of the tribes might turn back. To assure them, he told them that Banu Qurayza, the only Jewish tribe who had not yet broken the peace agreement, were now willing to help them. They will cut off the food and water supply to the Muslims and open the gates of Madinah. Surely then the Muslims will be defeated.

Huyay then went to the chief of Banu Qurayza, Ka'b Ibn Asad, to persuade him to break the agreement with the Prophet and the Muslims. At first, Ka'b refused to listen to him, but eventually, like all the other previous Jewish tribes, they agreed to help the Quraish and the Jews in defeating the Muslims.

When this news reached the Prophet he sent Sa'd Ibn Mu'adh and two others to Banu Qurayza to find out if the news was indeed true. Upon finding that the news was correct, Sa'd Ibn Mu'adh tried to persuade Banu Qurayza to stand by their agreement, but they refused to listen.

The Faith of the Muslims is Tested

The Muslims were now in a very serious and dangerous situation. Not only were they surrounded by enemies from the outside, but also under threat from enemies on the inside. Not for one moment could they relax their guard. Those Muslims who had true faith realised that this was the moment of trial and were ready to die for the cause of Islam. On the other hand, those of little and weak faith, such as the hypocrites, were in a state of panic and fear. Their condition is beautifully described by the Qur'an:

Being miserly towards you (as regards help and aid in Allah's Cause). Then when fear comes, you will see them looking to you with their eyes revolving.

166

Like one who faints from death, but when the fear has passed, they will smite
you with sharp tongues, miserly towards (spending anything in any) good.
Such men have no faith and so Allah has made their deeds fruitless; and that is
ever easy for Allah.

(Al Ahzab 33 :v 19)

Nuaym's Plot to Defeat the Quraish

Nu'aym was the person who was sent by Abu Sufyan to the
Muslims to persuade them not to march towards the Second Badr.
Nu'aym was also the person who had accepted Islam whilst on his
mission (this fact was unknown to the Quraish and the Jews).

Nu'aym decided to use this advantage in order to fight the Quraish.
After seeking permission from the Prophet, he went to speak to
Ka'b, chief of Banu Qurayza who were his former allies. He told
Ka'b that the Makkan army and the other Jewish tribes were
growing impatient because of this long wait. He questioned him:
"What would your fate be if the Makkan army returned to
Makkah?" He advised them that they should not fight on the side
of the Quraish until the Quraish sent them some hostages. If the
Quraish agreed, then surely they would not retreat back to Makkah
knowing that Banu Qurayza have some of their men. Ka'b agreed
to this suggestion, believing that Nu'aym was concerned about
their welfare.

Nu'aym then went to the Quraish and told them that he had some
confidential information. He said to Abu Sufyan: "Banu Qurayza
have regretted breaking the agreement with the Prophet
Muhammad and they are now willing to please him in any way.

167

They will ask you to give them some hostages and then they will kill them in order to please Muhammad. So if they ask you for hostages, you know what to think."

Abu Sufyan decided to test Nuaym's word. He sent a messenger to Ka'b Ibn Akhtab, telling him they would attack the Muslims immediately and needed help from Banu Qurayza. Ka'b told the messenger that the following day was a Saturday and that Elohim curses people who work on Saturdays. He then demanded some hostages. The messenger brought back this reply to Abu Sufyan who was now in no doubt that Nuaym's warning was valid. Feeling that they had already lost a great amount of time, four weeks in fact, he decided that they would attack Madinah the following morning.

The Storm and the Retreat of the Quraish

The situation looked desperate for the Muslims. The Prophet prayed to Allah to help the Muslims defeat their enemies. In answer to the Prophet's supplication, that very night a ferocious storm pulled down the tents of the Quraish and killed most of their camels and horses. Unseen hands began to batter and fight them. Some were attacked by their own animals. This continued for three days and three nights.

On the third day of the storm, Hudhayfah Ibn Yaman who had been sent across to the Quraish camp to observe their actions, overheard Abu Sufyan saying: "O men of Quraish we are in a very hostile situation. The storm has killed our animals, Banu Qurayza have broken their agreement with us and we have suffered a severe loss during the storm. So let us return to Makkah."

Sure enough, that very day the Quraish retreated back to Makkah on foot, taking with them what they could carry. The greatest and biggest army that the Arabs have ever gathered against the Muslims was now returning in a humiliated manner and in defeat.

The following morning, it was evident to the Muslims that the Quraish had retreated in defeat towards Makkah. The Qur'an says:

When they came upon you from above you and from below you, and when
the eyes grew wild and the hearts reached to the throats, and you were
harbouring doubts about Allah. There the believers were tried and shaken with
a mighty shaking. And when the hypocrites and those in whose hearts is a
disease (of doubts) said: "Allah and His Messenger promised us nothing but
delusions."
(Al Ahzab 33 :v 10-12)

Allah had tested the Muslims, but in the end He saved them from an unequal and unfair battle.

Siege of Banu Qurayza

Immediately after this victory, in which only ten Muslims had lost their lives, Angel Jibrail came to the Prophet Muhammad and said:

169

"O Messenger of God, you have laid down your arms but my angels have not. O Muhammad, go and punish Banu Qurayza for betraying you. They cannot be trusted nor allowed to remain inside the city walls."

An army was gathered and the Prophet ordered them to march against Banu Qurayza. The Muslims besieged them for twenty five days until they finally surrendered. They then asked the Prophet to let someone judge the case. He gave them the permission to choose who the judge should be.

They chose Sa'd Ibn Mu'adh, leader of the Aws, a tribe which had always protected the Qurayza in the past. They chose the man who had come to warn them not to break the agreement with the Muslims. Before judging the case Sa'd made both parties (Prophet Muhammad and Banu Qurayza) sign and swear to accept his decision. He decided that Banu Qurayza should be punished according to their law, in accordance with the Torah. They were all to be put to death except the women and children who were to be made captives.

The Prophet did not revoke this decision as he had earlier sworn to abide by it, but he did make one request. He requested that families should not be separated and thus taught his companions: 'He who separates mother and child shall be separated from those he loves in the eternal life.' Before being punished, the men of Banu Qurayza were offered to accept Islam. Only four accepted and the rest refused.

Very soon after this expedition, Sa'd Ibn Mu'adh died of wounds he received during the battle to defend Madinah. As it happened, the Angel Jibrail came to the Prophet in the middle of the night and said: "O Muhammad! Who is this dead man? When he arrived, the doors of Paradise opened and the Throne of Allah shook?"

Indeed if the Quraish and Jews had succeeded in their plan, Islam would have been destroyed and wiped off the face of the earth. Instead, from that day on, Madinah became a city where only Muslims lived.

Banu Al Mustaliq

The Muslims enjoyed some peace for a time, except for a few small attacks from Arab tribes. One of the most notable attack was that of Banu Al Mustaliq. They were making preparations to attack Madinah, but the Muslims had already been informed about this. They attacked Banu Al Mustaliq, who were completely taken by surprise and thus could not attack nor defend. The Muslims turned out victorious.

Case of Tu'ma and the Jew

When any case or dispute arose, be it small or big, the Prophet Muhammad was always asked to decide and judge.

In one such case, a man named Tu'ma stole a plate that was in a sack of wheat. He took the sack and hid it in the house of a Jew. Since the sack had a hole in it, the wheat kept falling out of the sack, all the way to the Jew's house. The owner of the sack, when realising it was stolen traced the track of wheat to the Jewish house and immediately reported the case to Prophet Muhammad. The Prophet enquired about the matter. Tu'ma claimed that the Jew had stolen it and the Jew claimed that Tu'ma had stolen it and had hid it in his house.

The tribe of Tu'ma came to defend him. They assured the Prophet that the Jew had committed the crime and begged him to defend Tu'ma. Looking at the evidence, the strongest being that the sack was traced and found in the house of the Jew, it seemed that the Jew would be unjustly punished. The Prophet was on the verge of defending Tu'ma when the following verses were revealed:

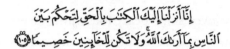

Surely, We have sent down to you the Book in truth that you might judge between men by that which Allah has shown you, so be not a pleader for the treacherous.

(An Nisa 4 : v 105)

إِنَّآ أَنزَلْنَآ إِلَيْكَ ٱلْكِتَٰبَ بِٱلْحَقِّ لِتَحْكُمَ بَيْنَ ٱلنَّاسِ بِمَآ أَرَىٰكَ ٱللَّهُ وَلَا تَكُن لِّلْخَآئِنِينَ خَصِيمًا ۝

وَلَوْلَا فَضْلُ ٱللَّهِ عَلَيْكَ وَرَحْمَتُهُ لَهَمَّت طَّآئِفَةٌ مِّنْهُمْ أَن يُضِلُّوكَ وَمَا يُضِلُّونَ إِلَّآ أَنفُسَهُمْ وَمَا يَضُرُّونَكَ مِن شَىْءٍ وَأَنزَلَ ٱللَّهُ عَلَيْكَ ٱلْكِتَٰبَ وَٱلْحِكْمَةَ وَعَلَّمَكَ مَا لَمْ تَكُن تَعْلَمُ وَكَانَ فَضْلُ ٱللَّهِ عَلَيْكَ عَظِيمًا ۝

Had not the Grace of Allah and His Mercy been upon you, a party of them would certainly have made a decision to mislead you, but they mislead none except their own selves. And no harm can they do to you in the least. Allah has sent down to you the Book and Al Hikmah. And taught you that which you knew not. And ever great is the grace of Allah unto you.

(An Nisa 4 :v 113)

The Prophet Muhammad reminded the companions that Allah has destroyed people because if the noble and honoured among them did wrong, they were not punished. But if the poor and weak among them did wrong, they were punished.

THE TREATY OF HUDAYBIYA

Muslims Go to Makkah

Six years had elapsed since the Muslims of Makkah had emigrated to Madinah. During these years, Islam had grown and spread. The number of Muslims increased day by day. The army increased from three hundred and thirteen (313) at the battle of Badr, to seven hundred (700) at the battle of Uhud and three thousand (3,000) at the battle of the Trench.

The desire to see their native city of Makkah was still there in-spite of all they had suffered at the hands of their fellow Makkans. Makkah was still dear to the hearts of the Emigrant Muslims and there were many who longed to visit their old homes. It so happened around this time, that the Prophet had a dream which indicated that the Muslims should go to Makkah for pilgrimage. Surely the Makkans could not refuse entry to Makkah for the Muslims. Even according to the customs of the Makkans, anybody who wishes to come to Makkah for the purpose of worshipping, may do so.

One thousand and four hundred (1400) Muslims prepared to go to Makkah with the Prophet for Umrah (small pilgrimage). They dressed in white and went unarmed. The Prophet assured the Quraish that they had no intention of fighting. But when the Quraish heard this news they sent an army under the command of Khalid Ibn Walid to confront the Muslims and stop them from entering Makkah. They could not allow Muhammad to enter Makkah for the sake of their prestige.

The Prophet and the pilgrims marched on until they reached 'Usfan', a place near Makkah. There they met a man from Banu Kalb who informed them of the approaching Quraish army. He told them that the Quraish have sworn by Allah that neither Muhammad nor any of the other pilgrims would enter Makkah.

Upon receiving this news the Prophet said: "Woe unto the Quraish. War has exhausted them. What do they lose if they leave me to the rest of the Arabs? If they defeat me, then this is what they want. If they do not, then the Quraish will enter Islam with honour. By Allah I shall continue to struggle for what I was sent until Allah makes it prevail or until this collar bone is severed (meaning until death)."

To avoid meeting the approaching army the Prophet changed his route and led the pilgrims through mountain passes. When they reached Hudaybiya, a place south of Makkah, the Prophet's camel refused to go any further. The Prophet commented: "The same power that once stopped the elephants from entering Makkah is now stopping us." The Muslims decided to camp at Hudaybiya with the intention of visiting Makkah the following morning.

Urwa Ibn Mas'ud

A camp was subsequently set up, but the Muslims were to hear some bad news: the springs were almost dry. The Prophet instructed a man named Najiyah to take the bowl of water in which he had performed his ablution and pour the contents into the dry spring, and stir it with his arrow. No sooner had he done this, fresh water began pouring out of the spring.

An emissary was sent to the Prophet on behalf of the Quraish. The mission of the emissary was to find out whether the Muslims would attack Makkah if they had the chance. His name was Urwa Ibn Mas'ud. He was a man of judgement and was known for his keen perception. He went to the Prophet and suggested to him that since the Muslims had changed their route to avoid meeting the army, which was now quite far away from Makkah, the gates of Makkah were wide open and undefended. Urwa said: "Makkah is an egg peeled in your hand."

From the view point of the Muslims this situation was an opportunity to attack Makkah, invade Makkah and humiliate the Quraish. But by his nature and by the teaching of Allah, the Prophet was truthful and told Urwa that he had come as pilgrim and not to fight. As a pilgrim he was seeking permission to enter Makkah.

Urwa returned to the Quraish impressed as well as touched and said: "I have seen Chosroes of Persia, Caesar in his dominion, Negus in his kingdom, but I have never seen a people who love their leader as the Muslims love Muhammad."

A messenger was sent to the Quraish by the Prophet to convince them that they came as pilgrims and not fighters. But Alas! The Quraish killed the messenger's camel and would also have killed him had not an Abyssinian interfered. On another occasion the Muslims caught fifty Quraish who tried to attack the Muslim camp and brought them before the Prophet who set them free, thus stressing the fact that the Muslims had not come to fight or take captives.

Uthman Ibn Affan is Sent to the Quraish

In a final attempt to convince the Quraish, the Prophet sent Uthman Ibn Affan, who was his son in law and a wise respected man, to the Quraish. Uthman, before becoming a Muslim was one of the greatest men amongst the Quraish.

On entering Makkah, Uthman Ibn Affan met Ahan Ibn Sa'id and asked him to be responsible for his life and safety during his stay in Makkah while negotiating with the Quraish. Ahan agreed to this.

When negotiating with the Quraish they told him that he could perform the pilgrimage if he wished to do so, but the Prophet Muhammad could not do so as they had sworn by Allah that Muhammad could not enter Makkah.

These negotiations took a considerable length of time and a rumour soon began to spread in the Muslim camp that Uthman had been killed. This was too much, even for the Prophet who said: "We shall not leave without fighting them." The Prophet then gathered all the Muslims under a tree and asked them to swear allegiance to fight to the death, even though they had no arms, shields, camels or horses. This pact later became known as the 'Bayat Al Rawdan' (Treaty of Paradise).

Shortly afterwards, the Muslims learnt that Uthman Ibn Affan was safe and alive and was delayed because of the lengthy negotiations with the Quraish. When he arrived in person, the Muslims were relieved. He told the Muslims that although the Quraish were convinced that they had not come to fight, they would not allow them to enter Makkah for the sake of their pride and prestige.

The rumour that Uthman had been killed in Makkah had actually been a test for the Muslims. It was a test to see whether the Muslims would fight without weapons, and whether they would depend on Allah or whether they still depended on material protection. The Qur'an says:

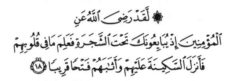

Indeed, Allah was pleased with the believers when they gave their Bay'ah (pledge) to you under the tree. He knew what was in their hearts, and sent down As sakinah (calmness and tranquillity) upon them, and rewarded them with a near victory.

(Al Fath 48 : v 18)

Treaty is Accepted

Soon after this, official messengers came from the Quraish and talks began for a peaceful settlement. One of the leaders of the Quraish, Suhayl Ibn Amr was sent to undertake these negotiations and work out a treaty. He was aggressive and discourteous in addressing Prophet Muhammad. When the Prophet asked Ali to write 'In the name of Allah, the Most Merciful, the Most Compassionate' on top of the page. Suhayl objected by saying: "Write only 'In your name O Allah'. I don't know Him as the Most Merciful and the Most Compassionate." The Prophet agreed and dictated: "This is a treaty between Muhammad the Messenger of Allah and Suhayl Ibn Amr." Again Suhayl objected. He remarked that he did not believe

Muhammad to be the Messenger of Allah, hence Muhammad should be referred in the treaty as 'Muhammad the son of Abdullah'. The Prophet accepted all this in tolerance and with great forbearance but the Muslims were outraged, especially Umar who said: "Are you not Allah's Messenger? Are we not Muslims? How can we accept this when we are right and they are wrong?" But the Prophet knew that what he was doing was for the best and signed.

The treaty included the following conditions:

1. The Muslims would return to Madinah without performing the Umrah.

2. The Muslims would perform Umrah the following year but only for three days.

3. On their visits to Makkah, the Muslims would not carry arms except for their swords.

4. There would be peace for ten years. Muslims would be allowed to go to Makkah and Taif and the Quraish could go to places such as Syria via Muslim areas.

5. Any Makkans taking refuge in Madinah would have to be returned to Makkah, on the demand of the Quraish. But if any Muslim took refuge in Makkah, the Quraish would not be under any compulsion to return him.

6. In cases of wars between other tribes, the Quraish and the Muslims would remain neutral.

7. The Muslims and the Quraish would be allowed to make and sign agreements with other Arab tribes.

To the Muslims, this treaty was a one-sided biased treaty favouring the Quraish, but later events proved that this treaty was actually a clear victory for the Muslims. As the Muslims were returning to Madinah disheartened and discouraged, the following verses were revealed:

إِنَّا فَتَحْنَا لَكَ فَتْحًا مُّبِينًا ۞ لِّيَغْفِرَ لَكَ اللَّهُ مَا تَقَدَّمَ مِن ذَنبِكَ وَمَا تَأَخَّرَ وَيُتِمَّ نِعْمَتَهُ عَلَيْكَ وَيَهْدِيَكَ صِرَاطًا مُّسْتَقِيمًا ۞ وَيَنصُرَكَ اللَّهُ نَصْرًا عَزِيزًا ۞

Verily We have given you a manifest victory. That Allah may forgive you your sins of the past and the future, and complete His favour on you and guide you on the Straight Path. And that Allah may help you with strong help.

(Al Fath 48 : v 1-3)

Upon the revelation of these verses, the Muslims were overjoyed. The verses combined forgiveness, hope, help, assurance and fulfilment.

The reason why the Qur'an describes this treaty as a 'manifest victory' was proven in later events. The treaty stopped war between the two parties. The Muslims in Makkah could come and live in Madinah. For all these years the Muslims had not been able to preach and spread Islam freely, but the Hudaybiya treaty allowed them to do so and as a result the whole of the Arabian Peninsula was lit up by the words of Allah. Thousands of Arabs embraced Islam. It was also during this period that Khalid Ibn Walid and Amr Ibn al Aas became Muslims. The former later became the most famous general in Islamic history and the latter became the conqueror of Egypt. As well as this, the Hudaybiya treaty opened the way for the conquest of Makkah in 630 CE, in the 8th year after the Hijrah.

Invitations To Islam

Since the peace treaty guaranteed peace for ten years, the Prophet decided that the time had come to spread the message of Islam to other countries. He sent his companions with letters inviting the rulers of the countries to Islam.

Letters were sent to Negus of Abyssinia, Himyrine of Yemen, Muqawqis of Egypt, Heraclius, the Roman Emperor and Chosroes of Persia. The contents of the letters called for the worship of one God alone. They informed the rulers that Islam was the road to salvation and peace. Each of the rulers responded according to his own respective manner and his understanding of the Truth.

Negus of Abyssinia
The Negus of Habasha (Abyssinia) was deeply moved by the letter and responded warmly. His reply was that he already considered himself to be a Muslim and believed that Muhammad was the Prophet of Allah. The Prophet sent another letter seeking permission for the Muslims who had emigrated to Abyssinia in the days of persecution, to return to Makkah. The Negus agreed and most of the Muslims returned to Makkah under the leadership of Ja'far Ibn Abu Talib.

Muqawqis of Egypt

Muqawqis of Egypt responded in a friendly manner and showed respect for the Prophet's letter. His main fear was that the people of Egypt would not accept this new message and thus he would be an insecure position if he became a Muslim. He also sent back with the messenger many gifts to the Prophet including a white mule.

Heraclius of Rome

Heraclius, the Roman Emperor, responded in a completely different manner. He did not question the messenger who had brought the letter, but sought out Arabs in his land. He found Abu Sufyan with a delegation which was there for commercial purposes. Abu Sufyan and his delegation were brought before Heraclius. Heraclius then began to question Abu Sufyan

After questioning Abu Sufyan, Heraclius concluded on the basis of the answers that Muhammad is a member of a respected family. He is trustworthy and has never been accused of lying or cheating. No-one has ever had any cause to doubt him or find fault with his reasoning. His followers increase day by day. He has never broken any agreement nor has he ever betrayed anyone. Heraclius concluded the meeting with these words: "He is indeed a Prophet and his followers do not leave him, which proves they have true faith, for faith does not enter the heart and go away. I knew from a dream I had that he was coming and he will surely conquer me. If I were with him now, I would have washed his feet."

Fearing that his people would turn against him and kill him, Heraclius asked Dihyah, the messenger, to take the letter to Bishop of Daghatir, whose words he said 'are more respected than mine.'

Dihyah went to the Bishop of Daghatir who immediately accepted it. He gathered the Romans in the church and said: "O Romans! A letter has come from Ahmad (Prophet Muhammad's name as mentioned in the Bible) in which he calls us to Allah. I bear witness that there is no divinity but Allah and Ahmad is His slave and Messenger." Upon hearing this, the crowd got outraged to the extent that they attacked the Bishop and beat him to death. Heraclius feared that the same thing would happen to him if he accepted Islam and thus sent a reply letter to the Prophet informing him of the situation.

Chosroes of Persia

Chosroes Parvez of Persia reacted angrily when he read Prophet Muhammad's letter. He tore the letter into pieces. Later when the Prophet heard what Chosroes had done, he said: "May Allah tear his Kingdom into pieces." A few days later Chosroes was killed by his own son. After that, the Persian throne was succeeded by one emperor after another in a matter of a few months. The Persian Empire continued to decline and weaken until it was eventually conquered by the Muslims during the Caliphate of Umar Ibn Al Khattab.

Although it was only Al Mundhir (king) of Bahrain and the Negus of Abysinnia who responded in the affirmative and became Muslims, a few years later Persia, Syria and Egypt all became Islamic States.

Banu Khaybar are Besieged

The Jews who had been expelled from Madinah went to live in

Khaybar, a prosperous town in Arabia. It was rich in crops and date groves. It was also a stronghold of the Jews which had seven fortresses.

Every Jewish tribe had broken the agreement made with the Prophet. They now gathered forces from tribes such as Banu Ghatafan who were known for their military strength. The Jews looked upon the Muslims as their greatest enemies. On the other hand, the Muslims looked upon Khaybar as the centre of anti-Islamic activities.

When the Muslims returned from Hudaybiya, a few skirmishes took place with the Jews of Khaybar. The Prophet decided to take action against the Jews of Khaybar upon receiving revelation commanding him to do so.

The Prophet marched towards Khaybar with an army of one thousand and five hundred (1500) men. Meanwhile the Jews of Khaybar thought that Prophet Muhammad and his army were no match for them. They had everything an army could want. However, to others, the result of the war was so unpredictable that the Quraish even made bets as to who would win. But the Muslims knew that Allah would protect them as they had complete trust in Him.

The Muslims started attacking Khaybar with the usual instruction of how to conduct themselves in the battle. They were not to kill women or children and older men. Houses and fields were not to be burnt.

The first three forts were besieged easily, but it was at the fourth fort that the Muslims struggled. The Prophet had asked Abu Bakr to force the gate open. Both he and other companions tried their utmost but could not break the gate. The next day Umar Ibn Al Khattab was sent to tackle the same task. Even brave Umar failed. On the third day, the Prophet sent Ali Ibn Abu Talib, with a flag and said to him: "Take this flag and go forth until Allah grants you victory. Offer them Islam before attacking the fortress."

The Jews refused to accept Islam and thus Ali Ibn Abu Talib started fighting them, displaying great bravery and courage. Once, during the fight, a Jew struck his shield away. Ali grabbed a door of the fort and used it as a shield until the fort was besieged and the Jews surrendered. Such was the bravery of this young man.

Abu Ra'fi, who was with Ali during this victory, reported later that he and seven others had tried to turn over the door that Ali had used as a shield but could not succeed. Ali was surely supported by a divine hand.

Downfall of the Jews

After their defeat, the Jews pleaded with the Prophet not to expel them from Khaybar and offered to remain on the land and cultivate palms for the Muslims. The Prophet made an agreement with them, that they were to give the Muslims half of the harvest each year and they were to stay on a temporary basis only. If the need arose, they would have to leave Khaybar.

When Abdullah Ibn Rawha used to go to the Jews to collect the

Muslim's share of the harvest, he always asked the Jews to take their share first. For incidents such as these, the Jews praised the Muslims for their justice and trustworthiness.

Other tribes made similar agreements with the Prophet, such as the Jews of Faddack and Wadil-Qura. The people of Thihama made an agreement to pay the defence tax *(jizya)* in order to remain on the land.

From this point onwards the Jews lost their land, power, influence and political status all over the Arabian Peninsula. All their efforts, individually and collectively, to destroy Islam had failed.

The lands that the Muslims had gained were distributed amongst the poor. The income from the land was used in freeing slaves and furthering the cause of Islam. Umar Ibn Al Khattab gained a plot of land and was wondering how the poor could benefit from it. The Prophet advised him to keep the land but to give away his yearly income to the poor. This is the first gift of its type in the history of Islam and there were many more to come.

Muslims Go to Makkah for Umrah

One year had passed since the signing of the Hudaybiya Treaty. The Muslims now had a right to enter Makkah as pilgrims for three days according to the treaty. The Prophet set out towards Makkah with thousands of Muslims. They were all unarmed except for their sheathed swords.

On arrival in Makkah at the Ka'bah, the Muslims called out: "We

come in answer to You, Our Lord! We come in answer to You."
They had arrived in hope and fear and now their hope had been
fulfilled and their fear had vanished. When the Prophet reached the
Ka'bah, he said: "My Lord have mercy upon a man who has let
them see strength in him today."

After going around the Ka'bah seven times, the Prophet went to
mount Safa and Marwa, the Muslims followed by example.

The Prophet and the Muslims remained in Makkah for three days
and three nights. They visited their homeland and relatives while
the Ansar were treated as honourable guests. An atmosphere of
enjoyment, happiness, reunion and optimism was felt all around.

Harith Ibn Umayr is Killed

Approximately three months after the Prophet's return from
Makkah, in the 8th year of Hijrah, the attention of the Muslims
was drawn to an Arab Christian state on the Arabian border with
Syria. The Prophet had sent Harith Ibn Umayr to that area to
deliver a letter inviting Shurahbil, chief of the Busra State, to Islam.
Shurahbil responded by killing Harith Ibn Umayr.

THE BATTLE OF MUTA

Upon hearing this, the Prophet sent out an army of three thousand (3,000) men to Busra, led by Zayd Ibn Al Harith. If he was killed the banner was to be given to Jafar Ibn Abu Talib and if he fell, Abdullah Ibn Rawah, a poet, would be in charge. Khalid Ibn Walid also accompanied the Muslims in this battle. Before the army set out, the Prophet again reminded them not to kill women, children, old people or blind men and not to destroy houses or cut down trees.

When the Muslims arrived at Muta (in Al Sham), they received news that the enemy had learnt of their approach and were now gathering forces from all neighbouring tribes. Upon hearing this, the majority of the Muslims decided that they should inform the Prophet of the numbers of the enemy and await his decision. This plan would have been carried out had it not been for the intervention of Abdullah Ibn Rawah who cried out: "We do not fight by weapons and numbers but by the religion that Allah has bestowed upon us." These moving words changed the decision and the Muslim army of three thousand (3,000) men marched forward to face an army of two hundred thousand (200,000) men.

They met the Roman army on the borders of Balaqa and fierce fighting broke out. Zayd Ibn Al Harith led the Muslim army into attack knowing that it meant certain death, which would be rewarded by paradise. He fought until he was killed. Jafar Ibn Abu Talib took charge and fought courageously until he too was killed. His enemy first killed his horse and then fought him on foot. He cut Jafar's right hand off, so Jafar held the banner with his left hand

and when this was cut off, he held the banner with his upper arms until he was killed. Now it was the turn of Abdullah Ibn Rawah to lead the attack. As he held the banner he uttered this poem:

> I swear, my heart, thou shalt charge in,
> I swear I shall repel thee.

He led the Muslims into another attack and fought bravely until he too died a shaheed.

Khalid Ibn Walid - Sword of Allah

This time Khalid Ibn Walid took the banner with great determination and fearless courage. He sensed that the Muslims were beginning to lose control. He changed the position of the army and attacked the enemy from a different angle. Nine swords were broken in the hand of Khalid. Intense fighting continued until the armies separated for the night.

Khalid made his attacking plans during that night. He changed the position of the army again, placing the right wing of the army on the left and the centre in the place of the rear. The tactical plan that was given to the men in the rear was that they should make such noise by marching as to give the impression that a large army was on its way to strengthen the Muslims. The plan was completed and finalised before dawn.

The Roman army was completely bewildered. They saw faces which they had not seen before (due to the change of positions by the Muslims) and they heard great marching noises coming towards them. In a state of panic and fear they thought the Muslims had brought reinforcements from Madinah. Their fears were centred around the fact that they were certain they could defeat an army of three thousand, but how were they going to defeat this army which had now brought reinforcements? They decided to stop attacking and would not fight the Muslims anymore. Shortly afterwards, the Romans were relieved to see that the Muslims had withdrawn from their territory and were returning to Madinah.

By Divine Inspiration the Prophet was informed of the victory for the Muslims (as he had remained in Madinah). After one of the prayers, he went up in the pulpit, his eyes full of tears, and cried out three times: "The Gate of Good! Know you all that Zayd has fallen as a martyr; implore the mercy of Allah in his favour. Then Jafar and Abdullah died martyrs; implore the mercy of Allah for them. Then the standard was upheld by Khalid Ibn Walid who is the sword among all of the swords of Allah. And Almighty Allah granted him victory." From that day on Khalid Ibn Walid was known as 'Saifullah' (Sword of Allah).

Whilst consoling the family of Jafar, the Prophet suddenly lifted his head upwards and murmured: "The salvation and mercy of Allah be upon you." The companions asked as to who he was speaking to. "I have just seen Jafar go by in the midst of a procession of angels. He was entering Paradise with ruby studded wings instead of his amputated arms. He greeted me and I returned his greeting."

Suhail (who recorded this tradition) later added: "Those are merely images: the wings are symbolic of the supernatural strength

190

of Jafar's soul; and the rubies are the precious drops of his blood."

When the return of the army was announced, the whole population of Madinah went out to meet them. Some of them confronted the army asking why they had not slaughtered the enemy. But the Prophet gave the returning soldiers a warm welcome. He congratulated them on their courage and told them that the army deserved praise.

This was clearly a major victory for the Muslims and Islam. They had with the Divine Help of Allah, defeated an army which they had second thoughts about attacking. This battle was the first major encounter between Muslims and Romans.

Another positive result of this victory at Muta was that many Arab tribes witnessed the determination and courage of the Muslims against a Roman army which was far superior to them in every respect. Surely the message that the Muslims were carrying could not be false and yet prevail. Amongst the Arab tribes who entered Islam were Salman, Abbasa, Kazan and even Ghatafan who a few years ago were one of the major enemies of Islam. Indeed none can misguide whom Allah wishes to guide.

The Hudaybiya Treaty is Violated

The 8th year of Hijrah was drawing to a close. The Treaty of Hudaybiya had been in force for two consecutive years. One of the conditions of the treaty was that for a period of ten years there should be no attack by the Makkans on the Muslims nor should there be any attack by the Mulsims on the Makkans.

The Hudaybiya Treaty also gave freedom for the Quraish and the Muslims to make agreements with other tribes. Hence, the tribe of Banu Bakr became the allies of the Quraish, whilst the tribe of Banu Khuza'a sided with the Muslims.

A few months after the Muslim army had returned from the Battle of Muta, a rumour spread that they had been completely destroyed and were in a weak position. The Quraish heard of this and perceived this to be the moment to break the treaty without receiving any retaliation from the Muslims.

A plan was formulated and carried out accordingly. Members of Banu Bakr attacked some members of Banu Khuza'a while they were asleep, killing several of them. Even those who took refuge in the Ka'bah were butchered. The Quraish took no measures to prevent the attack and secretly helped their allies. Thus the Treaty of Hudaybiya had been violated by the Quraish. Forty men of Banu Khuza'a came to the Prophet to complain and seek assistance. The Prophet assured them that they would be helped.

Meanwhile the Quraish realised that they had miscalculated in their assesment of the situation. They were now fearing the action that was bound to be taken by Prophet Muhammad.

Abu Sufyan Goes to Madinah

The Prophet then sent word to the Quraish telling them to accept one of the following penalties due to their behaviour and untrustworthiness in breaking the treaty:

1. To pay compensation to the tribe of Khuza'a or
2. To withdraw support from Banu Bakr or
3. To declare the Treaty of Hudaybiya as no longer valid.

In reply, the chief of the Quraish, Abu Sufyan, foolishly decided to accept the last option. The Prophet was left with no choice but to attack the Quraish.

Later on, Abu Sufyan realised that he had made a mistake in choosing the last option. Out of fear, he decided to go to Madinah and make peace with the Prophet. Again, out of fear, he did not dare go to the Prophet himself, but he went to Umm Habiba, his daughter and the Prophet's wife. When Abu Sufyan was about to sit down on the rug that the Prophet slept on, Umm Habiba objected. In an offended manner he asked her whether he was unworthy of the bed or the bed was unworthy of him. She replied: "You are an idol worshipper and therefore in a state of impurity, and this is the Prophet's bed." Abu Sufyan commented: "O my daughter, some misfortune has happened bringing disorder to your mind since the day you left us."

Understanding by this kind of welcome that there was no hope for him in that quarter, he went to the Prophet in person. He offered peace and an extension of the Treaty of Hudaybiya for another ten years. The Prophet rose and left Abu Sufyan without saying a word. The Prophet did not want to mislead the Quraish nor did he want to declare war openly for he hoped to enter Makkah without bloodshed. The only way this could be achieved was to conquer Makkah by surprise.

Abu Sufyan then went to seek the help of Abu Bakr who was as firm as the Prophet had been. He then approached Umar and Ali and pleaded to them to intercede in favour of his fellow citizens. Upon hearing another negative answer, he mounted his camel and went back to Makkah, full of apprehension and in a state of humiliation.

The March Towards Makkah

Preparations began in Madinah. Ten thousand men were ready, and it was not until the very last moment that they knew they were conquering Makkah in surprise. The Prophet prayed to Allah to avoid bloodshed when entering Makkah.

At long last, on the 20th day of Ramadhan, in the 8th year after Hijrah, an army of ten thousand (10,000) marched towards Makkah and thus fulfilled the divine words which were spoken two thousand years before, through the lips of Prophet Musa: "He came with the ten thousand holy ones..." Their objective in life was not war, power or money, but it was the establishment of the worship of One Allah.

As they marched, many of the tribes who had recently entered Islam joined in and thus the numbers increased and increased as they approached Makkah.

Since it was the month of Ramadhan, the fasting was strictly observed by the Muslims, but when they reached the well of Al Khalid in the middle of the day, the Prophet judged that their faith had been sufficiently tested. Fearing that the deprivation of drink, along with extreme tiredness might have a dangerous effect on their health, he asked for a bowl of water. He drank a mouthful in front of the Muslims, so as to teach by his example that they may break their fast when on a journey as soon as they feel their strength weaken.

After this, the Prophet marched on with the army until they reached Marrudh Dhahran, a place close to the town gates of Makkah. It was here that they decided to camp. The Prophet ordered every man to kindle a fire in each camp in the hope that when the Makkans saw them, they will be shocked by the great numbers of the Muslim army and thus avoid fighting.

As a result of the secret preparations, the Quraish were yet unaware of what was happening. They were still arguing on what was to be done about Prophet Muhammad. The Prophet's uncle Al Abbas had left Makkah and was going to Madinah when he met the Muslims and the Prophet on the way.

When Al Abbas saw the enormous army accompanied with the Prophet, he was alarmed. Even though he was a Muslim, Makkah was his city and it would grieve him to see any harm come to it. The Prophet was pleased when his uncle talked to him about his concerns. He could now use Al Abbas as a means of entering Makkah in peace. It was agreed between the Prophet and his uncle, that the latter would return to Makkah and convince the Quraish that the Prophet and his followers would like to enter Makkah in peace. Al Abbas headed towards Makkah on a white mule.

As Al Abbas approached Makkah, two familiar voices were

speaking in the dark. He immediately recognised them as the voices of Budayl Ibn Waraqa and Abu Sufyan. The latter was saying: "I have never seen so many fires as I see tonight." Budayl suggested that they were the fires of Khuza'a, but Abu Sufyan disagreed: "Khuza'a are not so enormous. Those fires cannot be theirs."

At this point, Al Abbas made his presence known and addressed Abu Sufyan: "O Abu Sufyan! The fires you see are those of the Muslims. They have brought with them a large army but they do not wish to fight. They only want to enter Makkah in peace. It would be better to surrender and not fight. Come under my protection and meet Prophet Muhammad." Abu Sufyan realising that this was his last hope of safety, could only submit. He got up behind Al Abbas on the white mule.

As they travelled through the Muslim camp, they were stopped at each camp-fire and a guard would shout out: "Who goes here?" On realising it was Al Abbas they would let him pass through. No one had recognised Abu Sufyan at the back of the white mule due to the darkness of the night, but when they passed Umar, he immediately recognised Abu Sufyan and cried out: "Abu Sufyan! The enemy of Allah is here!" He ran towards the mule with the intention of killing him, but the mule was made to go faster and Umar was unable to catch them.

When Al Abbas and Abu Sufyan reached the Prophet's tent, Umar rushed in and pleaded with the Prophet to allow him to end the life of Abu Sufyan, the arch enemy of Islam. Al Abbas intervened and said that Abu Sufyan was under his protection. Thus the Prophet asked his uncle to bring Abu Sufyan to him the following morning.

Abu Sufyan Enters Islam

It appeared simply impossible that the Prophet would forgive Abu Sufyan. Time and again, he had tried his utmost to crush Islam and many Muslims were killed at his hands. But the Prophet's merciful nature was extended to friend and foe alike. Abu Sufyan was forgiven and after twenty long years his heart was opened to the Truth. He embraced Islam and declared his belief without reservation. The Prophet then told Abu Sufyan to return to Makkah and inform the Quraish that the Muslims would enter the city the following morning. Before his departure, Al Abbas made a request to the Prophet that as Abu Sufyan was a proud man, it would be good to give him an honourable position. The Prophet took his uncle's advice and said to Abu Sufyan: "Tell your people that he who enters the house of Abu Sufyan is safe, he who enters his own house is safe and he who enters the area of the Ka'bah is safe."

Such was the merciful nature of the Prophet that he bore no grudges against the polytheists of Makkah and was willing not only to forgive, but also to honour his former enemies.

THE CONQUEST OF MAKKAH

The Prophet divided the army into four groups. Each was to enter Makkah from a different direction. They had been ordered to cause no harm unless anyone tried to stop them entering.

On approaching Makkah, the Prophet realised that there was no sign of retaliation on behalf of the Quraish and thanked Allah for this peaceful entry without bloodshed. However, he was very saddened when news reached him that one of the four groups had met opposition and lives were lost on both sides. The leader of that group was Khalid Ibn Walid. Other than this small but painful incident, there were no other attack on the Muslims.

As the Prophet passed through the long winding streets of Makkah, his mind wondered back to the days when he was simply an inhabitant of the city. In the hour of this victory, he felt the absence of many loved companions, above all Khadijah.

The Muslims of Makkah returned to their own homes and families. A tent was erected for the Prophet by the grave of his grandfather and that of Khadijah, who had been with him for twenty-five years. He remained praying in the tent, then he encircled the Ka'bah seven times on his camel. He then addressed the people around him: "There is no divinity except Allah and He has no partner. Men and women of Quraish, be not proud for all are equals. We are all sons of Adam and Adam was created from dust." He then recited the following verses:

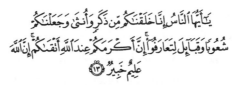

O Mankind! We have created you from a male and a female, and made you
into nations and tribes so that you may know one another. Verily, the most
honourable of you in the Sight of Allah is that (believer) who has At Taqwa.
Verily, Allah is All-Knowing, All Aware.

(Al Hujurat 49 : v 13)

The Quraish are Forgiven

The Quraish were then addressed. They had all come to see what
their fate would be. What would the man they had tortured,
abused, injured, and harassed, decide?

The Prophet looked at the Quraish, smiling and said: "O Quraish!
What do you think I shall do with you?" The Quraish pondered
and realised that according to the laws of war, they would all be
taken prisoners. However, they also knew the Prophet Muhammad
to be merciful by nature, so they replied: "You will treat us as a kind
nephew and a generous brother would." To this the Prophet
replied: "God forgives you and He is the Most Merciful of the
Merciful." The Quraish were bewildered. They had come fearing
the worst, but instead they returned with the best.

The Prophet then went to Mount Safa and the crowd followed
him. They surged forward, taking his hand one by one, to declare
themselves as Muslims.

In order to enter the Ka'bah, Ali Ibn Abu Talib went to the

custodians of the Ka'bah and claimed the keys by force because the man, who was still a polytheist, had protested, saying that if he knew Muhammad to be the Messenger of Allah, he would have given the keys himself to the Prophet Muhammad.

The entrance was opened and the Prophet entered the Ka'bah. Inside he saw pictures of Prophets as old men and angels as beautiful women on the wall. He asked the paintings to be erased from the wall. The Prophet then took his staff and broke idol after idol, three hundred and sixty five in total. As he was doing so, he recited the following verses:

وَقُلْ جَآءَ ٱلْحَقُّ وَزَهَقَ ٱلْبَـٰطِلُ إِنَّ ٱلْبَـٰطِلَ كَانَ زَهُوقًا ۝

And say: "Truth has come and Batil (falsehood) has vanished. Surely! Batil is ever bound to vanish."

(Al Isra 17 : v 81)

Thus the Ka'bah was now free from idol worship and returned to its true and original purpose of worshipping Allah alone.

After completing his duties at the Ka'bah, the Prophet returned the keys to the polytheist custodian, who was completely bewildered by this and asked for an explanation. The Prophet in answer recited the following verses:

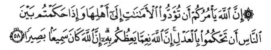

إِنَّ ٱللَّهَ يَأْمُرُكُمْ أَن تُؤَدُّوا۟ ٱلْأَمَـٰنَـٰتِ إِلَىٰٓ أَهْلِهَا وَإِذَا حَكَمْتُم بَيْنَ ٱلنَّاسِ أَن تَحْكُمُوا۟ بِٱلْعَدْلِ إِنَّ ٱللَّهَ نِعِمَّا يَعِظُكُم بِهِۦٓ إِنَّ ٱللَّهَ كَانَ سَمِيعًا بَصِيرًا ۝

Verily, Allah commands that you should render back the trusts to those to whom they are due. And that when you judge between men, you judge with justice. Verily, how excellent is the teaching which He (Allah) gives. Truly Allah is Ever All-Hearer, All Seer.

(An Nisa 4 :v 58)

Talha, the polytheist custodian, accepted Islam due to this action by the Prophet and the key remained a sacred trust.

The Ansar are Worried

The Ansar of Madinah were with the Prophet during these times and feared that the Prophet Muhammad would not return with them to Madinah now that he could remain in the city of his birth safely. The Prophet once questioned them as to what they seemed to be worrying about. In a state of hesitancy and shyness they explained their worry.

The Prophet replied by saying: "Allah forbid, My life is with you and my death will be amongst you."

After all, he explained to them, they were the people who had opened their hearts, city and homes to him when everyone else was against him. They were the people who helped him build the Islamic State in Madinah. They were the people who fought courageously in lengthy wars. Of course, he could not leave them, even at the expense of leaving Makkah.

Quraish Accept Islam

Most of the Makkan Quraish accepted Islam of their own accord, be it men, women or children. Only four Makkans who had committed murder for personal reasons were put to death in accordance with the laws of Islam. The rest of the Quraish were forgiven.

The surrender of Makkah took place on Friday 25th of Ramadhan, in the 8th year after Hijrah, in the year 637 CE. For a month and a half, the Prophet stayed in Makkah to organise the affairs of the newly established Islamic government. Of course the implementation of all the Islamic laws was not done immediately, rather it was a gradual process.

Every day Bilal would sound the call to prayer. All the Muslims - emigrants, supporters, helpers, Makkans and the tribesmen would respond to the call. There was Peace. There was tranquillity. There was harmony. They were all brothers and sisters in Islam, united behind one cause: to worship only Allah.

Never in the history of the Arabs was there a time where all the Arab tribes and nations were united under one cause, except this.

BATTLE OF HUNAYN

The conquest of Makkah opened way for Islam to flourish and the Muslims grew stronger day by day. Not a week passed in which no tribe entered Islam. However, the tribe of Hawazin and Thaqif made an agreement that they would destroy Islam before it could conquer them and the whole of Arabia.

Once again, the Muslims prepared for another battle. But their position in this battle was different from all other previous battles. For the first time in their military history, the Muslims had more men, weapons, horse power, skill and experience than their enemy. Their army consisted of twelve thousand (12,000) soldiers, ten thousand (10,000) of whom were the conquerors of Makkah and the remaining two thousand (2,000) from the Quraish. Their enemy only had four thousand (4,000) soldiers.

The Muslim army marched towards Hunayn under the leadership of Khalid Ibn Walid and when they reached the valleys of Hunayn they camped for the night. Their morale was high. They were pleased with their numbers and they were very proud of their strength. They said to each other: "Today we are invincible, today we cannot lose and no-one is a match for us." The Prophet constantly reminded them to depend on Allah and not on their strength and numbers.

The time for the battle came. It was very early in the morning and not yet light. The Muslim army advanced along the Hunayn path which was a narrow path between two rugged mountains. They were not aware that the enemy had climbed these mountains and were waiting for the best possible moment to attack. Thus when they saw the Muslim army advancing along the narrow pathway, they ambushed them and took them completely by surprise. First they threw rocks down and then showered them with arrows.

The sudden attack spread a great panic amongst the Muslim ranks. They were terrified and thus fled in a disorderly manner. Confusion was the order of the day. The Prophet was bitterly disappointed to see them flee in terror. As they were fleeing, the Prophet caught sight of the man who was leading the enemy's attack. He rode forwards to attack this formidable enemy. However, one of the companions, upon realising that the Prophet may be injured if he went to attack the enemy who was on top of the mountain, held tight to the reigns of the Prophet's mule and thus prevented it from moving. Meanwhile, Al Abbas shouted out to the fleeing Muslims: "You emigrants who have sworn the oath under the tree! Muhammad is alive, so come back and do not abandon him."

This plea was repeated again and again until it reached the ears of the fleeing Muslims. Those who had sincere faith returned back to the battlefield; six hundred in all.

Those six hundred sincere Muslims attacked the army of four thousand men and were able to push them back. Surely Allah had sent His angels to the aid of the Muslims. As the battle progressed, the enemy began to retreat and the Muslims turned out victorious.

The Qur'an says:

لَقَدۡ نَصَرَكُمُ ٱللَّهُ فِى مَوَاطِنَ
كَثِيرَةٍ وَيَوۡمَ حُنَيۡنٍ إِذۡ أَعۡجَبَتۡكُمۡ كَثۡرَتُكُمۡ فَلَمۡ
تُغۡنِ عَنكُمۡ شَيۡئًا وَضَاقَتۡ عَلَيۡكُمُ ٱلۡأَرۡضُ
بِمَا رَحُبَتۡ ثُمَّ وَلَّيۡتُم مُّدۡبِرِينَ ﴿٢٥﴾ ثُمَّ أَنزَلَ ٱللَّهُ سَكِينَتَهُۥ
عَلَىٰ رَسُولِهِۦ وَعَلَى ٱلۡمُؤۡمِنِينَ وَأَنزَلَ جُنُودًا لَّمۡ تَرَوۡهَا
وَعَذَّبَ ٱلَّذِينَ كَفَرُواْ وَذَٰلِكَ جَزَآءُ ٱلۡكَٰفِرِينَ ﴿٢٦﴾

Truly Allah has given you victory on many battle-fields on the Day of Hunayn
when you rejoiced at your great number but it availed you naught and the
earth, vast as it is, was straitened for you, then you turned back in flight. Then
Allah sent down His Sakinah (calmness, tranquillity and reassurance, etc.) on
the Messenger, and on the believers, and sent down forces (angels) which you
saw not, and punished the disbelievers. Such is the recompense of disbelievers.

(At Tauba 9 v: 25-26)

The lesson that the Muslims learnt was similar to that of Uhud.
Victory comes from Allah and not from the number of men or
weapons. When the Muslims relied on their numbers, Allah
withdrew His Support. Surely this was a lesson that prepared and
cautioned the Muslims in the battles that were to follow.

Siege of Taif

A part of the defeated army, including the leaders of Hawazin and
Thaqif, took shelter behind the walls of Taif, so the Muslim army
surrounded the city. It was strongly guarded and there was no lack
of water or provisions within the walls. The Prophet concluded
after a considerable amount of thinking, that the only way to make
the enemy surrender without shedding blood was to burn the

palms situated on the fertile lands around Taif. The Prophet hated to do this, and had in the past ordered his followers to refrain from such actions. But he had no other choice. As soon as the palm trees were set on fire the enemy surrendered. The Prophet warned them not to attack the Muslims again and asked them to withdraw the army from Taif. Some of them were taken prisoners. Shortly afterwards, the tribe of Hawazin and Thaqif along with many other Arab tribes came to Makkah and accepted Islam.

Shaima: The Prophet's Foster Sister

On his return from Taif, the Prophet divided the booty amongst the Muslims, setting apart as usual, one fifth for the public treasury. Some of the prisoners had known the Prophet since he was a child. Among the women prisoners was a person named Shaima. As soon as the Prophet saw her he recognised her as being his foster sister. He spread his own mantle for her to seat herself upon and talked to her of those early days. She was at once released and sent back to her people with some presents.

Seeing the Prophet's kindness, the other prisoners begged him to set them free. They said: "We have known you as a child, then as a noble young man and now you are so great a man...be merciful to us." The Prophet's heart would melt at the sight of the smallest human misery and at once he released all the prisoners - six thousand (6,000) in total. This event stands unique in the history of the world.

Distribution of the Booty

The flocks, herds and various spoils of the war were distributed amongst the army. The Prophet gave presents to the chiefs of Arab tribes, some received as many as one hundred camels. The Ansar from Madinah received nothing and seeing how the Prophet had given generously to those newly entered into Islam who had previously been their enemies, they said to each other: "He has joined his own people and has forgotten us." When these words reached the Prophet, he called the Ansar and said to them: "O Helpers! You are disturbed because I have sought to win the hearts of the people of Makkah. But remember I came to you when I had none to help me, and you stood by me. O Helpers! Do you not like that you take home with you the Prophet of Allah, while others take goats and camels? By Allah! I will never leave you. If all men were to go one way, and the men of Madinah another, I would follow the men of Madinah."

This spontaneous outburst of the Prophet's heart shows how little weight worldly riches carried with him. The Helpers were deeply moved, many of them bursting into tears of joy. The Prophet stayed in Makkah until the 9th of Shawwal, in the 8th year after Hijrah, and then returned to Madinah.

Spread of Islam

Makkah was known as Umm al Qura, or the 'mother of towns', although it was not regarded as the capital of Arabia. During the months of pilgrimage, people from every part of the country used to gather there. Naturally, the people of Makkah had great influence over these people.

In the years 9 A.H. and 10 A.H. (After Hijrah) Islam spread over all Arabia and reached the borders of the Roman and Persian empires. This period of general acceptance of Islam began within the year 9 A.H., when tribe after tribe came into the fold of Islam. A separate establishment was organised for the purpose of dealing with the new situation and collectors were sent out to various places. The tribes who entered Islam paid the alms tax, which was an obligation on the Muslims. A defence tax was also paid by those tribes who had not yet entered Islam, in return for security of life and property.

Banu Tamim enters Islam

Banu Tamim were the tribe who had given assistance to the Prophet and the Muslims in the battle of Hunayn. They sent a delegation to Madinah to wait upon the Prophet. A controversial deabte was held between speakers and poets from both sides on the subject of religion. Finally, the tribe of Banu Tamim had to admit defeat and acknowledged the superiority of the Muslims and Islam. This time they accepted Islam knowing that this was the only way of life acceptable to Allah.

Deputation from Arab Tribes

Those people who attended the annual pilgrimage were very impressed by the behaviour and conduct of the Muslims. They knew that the Prophet and his followers had been brutally tortured, persecuted and killed and yet the Prophet took no revenge on anyone but forgave his enemies. This news began to spread to all parts of the country.

Deputations began to pour into Madinah from place such as Yemen, Bahrain, Ammán, Syria and Persia and every other part of the Arabian peninsula. The Prophet received them with great honour and taught them the principles of Islam. In cases where the tribes had to go back to their city, the Prophet sent a teacher with them to teach the principles of Islam.

CAMPAIGN OF TABUK

The Roman empire could not tolerate the increasing power and influence of the Muslims. When news reached them, that the whole of Arabia was giving allegiance to Islam, they were outraged. They had cherished the hope of converting Arabia to their own faith. They decided that an attack upon the country would at least minimise the spread of Islam.

News reached Madinah that Caesar had assembled a large force to crush the Muslims with the help of all the neighbouring Christian tribes. Once again the Muslims had to fight with arms to defend Islam. The Prophet had to collect and prepare an army to fight against this mighty force.

The best method of defence was to keep the enemy outside the boundaries of Arabia, thus an expedition needed to be sent. The Prophet summoned all the Muslim tribes to come and defend Islam and their motherland. The impending danger was threatening the peace of the whole of Arabia.

The Muslims are Tested

Everyone was asked to contribute in whatever way they could. The rich were to spend some of their wealth. Those who were fit to fight were told to join the army. In actual fact, the Muslims were being tested and when one is tested he or she always has to be faced with problems and obstacles. The obstacles in this case were that the journey was long and the weather was extremely hot. Crops were ripe and were ready to be harvested and above all, the main obstacle was the fear of facing the well-disciplined and trained forces of the Roman Empire. Regarding this, the Qur'an says:

يَـٰٓأَيُّهَا ٱلَّذِينَ
ءَامَنُوٓا۟ مَا لَكُمْ إِذَا قِيلَ لَكُمُ ٱنفِرُوا۟ فِى سَبِيلِ ٱللَّهِ ٱثَّاقَلْتُمْ
إِلَى ٱلْأَرْضِ أَرَضِيتُم بِٱلْحَيَوٰةِ ٱلدُّنْيَا مِنَ ٱلْأَخِرَةِ
فَمَا مَتَٰعُ ٱلْحَيَوٰةِ ٱلدُّنْيَا فِى ٱلْأَخِرَةِ إِلَّا قَلِيلٌ ۝

O you who believe! What is the matter with you, that when you are asked to march forth in the Cause of Allah(i.e. Jihad) you cling heavily to the earth? Are you pleased with the life of this world rather than the Hereafter? But little is the enjoyment of the life of this world as compared with the Hereafter.

(At Tauba 9 :v 38)

Those who were sincere were willing to risk their lives for the sake of Islam, regardless of any obstacles. They knew that they would have to travel for many days before they reached any source of food or water.

Those who were weak in faith and those who had accepted Islam for material considerations were reluctant to quit the ease and shelter of their homes and thus made up false excuses. Concerning these people, the Qur'an says:

وَمِنْهُم مَّن يَقُولُ ٱئْذَن لِّى وَلَا تَفْتِنِّىٓ أَلَا فِى ٱلْفِتْنَةِ
سَقَطُوا۟ وَإِنَّ جَهَنَّمَ لَمُحِيطَةٌۢ بِٱلْكَٰفِرِينَ ۝

And among them is he who says: "Grant me leave (to be exempted from Jihad) and put me not into trial." Surely, they have fallen into trial. And verily, Hell is surrounding the disbelievers.

(At Tauba 9 :v 49)

The hypocrites said to one another: "Don't go forth to war in this heat." Concerning this attitude of the hypocrites, the Qur'an says:

211

فَرِحَ الْمُخَلَّفُونَ
بِمَقْعَدِهِمْ خِلَفَ رَسُولِ اللَّهِ وَكَرِهُوٓا أَن يُجَٰهِدُوا بِأَمْوَٰلِهِمْ
وَأَنفُسِهِمْ فِى سَبِيلِ اللَّهِ وَقَالُوا لَا تَنفِرُوا فِى الْحَرِّ قُلْ نَارُ جَهَنَّمَ
أَشَدُّ حَرًّا لَّوْ كَانُوا يَفْقَهُونَ ۝ فَلْيَضْحَكُوا قَلِيلًا وَلْيَبْكُوا كَثِيرًا
جَزَآءًۢ بِمَا كَانُوا يَكْسِبُونَ ۝

Those who stayed away (from Tabuk expedition) rejoiced in their staying
behind from the Messenger of Allah; They hated to strive and fight with their
properties and their lives in the Cause of Allah, and they said: "March not
forth in the heat." Say: "The Fire of Hell is more intense in heat", if only they
could understand! So let them laugh a little and (they will) cry much as a
recompense of what they used to earn (by committing sins).
(At Tauba 9 : v 81-82)

Amongst the hypocrites, some of them not only stayed behind, but
actively encouraged others to do the same. The hypocrites used to
meet in the house of Suwaylim, a Jew, and conspire against the
Muslims. When this news reached the Prophet, he sent Talha Ibn
Ubaydullah to burn the house of Suwaylim in order to stop the
conspiracies of the hypocrites.

Among the sincere Muslims who were willing to fight and die for
the cause of Islam, some were very poor, sick and weak and thus
genuinely could not participate or join the army. They were so sad
that they were nicknamed the 'Bakkarun' or 'Weepers'.
Nevertheless, they are excused by the following Qur'anic statement:

بِسْمِ اللَّهِ الرَّحْمَنِ الرَّحِيمِ

لَيْسَ عَلَى الضُّعَفَاءِ وَلَا عَلَى الْمَرْضَى وَلَا عَلَى الَّذِينَ
لَا يَجِدُونَ مَا يُنفِقُونَ حَرَجٌ إِذَا نَصَحُوا لِلَّهِ وَرَسُولِهِ
مَا عَلَى الْمُحْسِنِينَ مِن سَبِيلٍ وَاللَّهُ غَفُورٌ رَّحِيمٌ ۝
وَلَا عَلَى الَّذِينَ إِذَا مَا أَتَوْكَ لِتَحْمِلَهُمْ قُلْتَ لَا أَجِدُ
مَا أَحْمِلُكُمْ عَلَيْهِ تَوَلَّوا وَّأَعْيُنُهُمْ تَفِيضُ مِنَ الدَّمْعِ
حَزَنًا أَلَّا يَجِدُوا مَا يُنفِقُونَ ۝

There is no blame on those who are weak or ill or who find no resources to
spend [in holy warfare (Jihad)], if they are sincere (in duty) to Allah and His
Messenger. No ground (of complaint) can there be against the Muhsinun
(good-doers). And Allah is Oft-Forgiving, Most Merciful. Nor (is there blame)
on those who came to you to be provided with mounts, and when you said: "I
can find no mounts for you," they turned back, with their eyes overflowing
with tears of grief that they could not find anything to spend (for Jihad).

(At Tauba 9 :v 91-92)

Despite the drawbacks from some parts of the Muslim
community, there were many who responded positively. Many of
the rich gave generously; Uthman Ibn Affan sent 10,000 dinars and
some weapons; Umar presented half of his total belongings; Abu
Bakr placed the whole of his fortune at the disposal of the Prophet
Muhammad who asked him: "O Abu Bakr! Have you left anything
for your family?" "I have left Allah and His Messenger," was the
reply. Abdul Rahman Ibn Awf brought two hundred ounces of
silver. The women contributed by giving some of their precious
ornaments.

Despite all the odds, despite all the obstacles, despite the
withdrawal of the hypocrites, an army of thirty thousand (30,000)
soldiers was finally assembled. At Badr there had only been three
hundred and thirteen (313), at Uhud seven hundred (700), at

Khaybar only two years ago, sixteen hundred (1600) and now thirty thousand (30,000). Because of the difficulties faced in organising the army, it was given the name of 'Jaysh Al Usra' or the 'hardship army'.

March towards Tabuk

In the month of Rajab 9 AH, the Prophet and the army of 30,000 marched towards Tabuk leaving Muhammad Ibn Maslamah in charge of Madinah, and Ali was appointed the guardian of the Prophet's household.

During the march, the heat was so intense and the journey so difficult that several Muslims turned back to Madinah. The Prophet and the rest of the army continued to march until they finally ran out of water. The Prophet prayed to Allah for help and no sooner had he finished, rain came pouring down from the sky.

Only did the rain stop, when all of the Muslims had drank to their fill. That night they slept soundly and without feeling thirsty for the first time in days and waited for the Adhan to wake them up. But as it happened, Bilal who was supposed to sound the call of prayer, had also slept deeply and did not wake up to give the Adhan. The Muslims were very upset that they had missed the dawn prayer. This was the first time that they had missed a prayer. But the Prophet consoled them by saying that since they did not intentionally miss the prayer, there was no reason to be upset.

The Romans Retreat

Midway between Madinah and Damascus, at a distance of fourteen (14) days journey from the latter, lies a place known as Tabuk. Here the Muslim army encamped and awaited news of the enemy. News reached them that the Romans had retreated back into their own territory upon learning of the strength of the Muslim army. The Romans had retreated even before they were involved in any fighting.

If conversion was to be secured at the point of the sword, could there have been a more promising opportunity than this? But not a single conversion is reported as a result of this expedition. The Muslims could even have gained territorial advantage. The lands of Syria and Damascus lay open before them as if inviting the Muslims to conquer it. But no, the Muslims killed no-one, converted no one by the sword and did not conquer any land. Is there a single event in history which can be compared to this event?

Treaties are Signed

After waiting for twenty days, the Prophet was satisfied that there was no cause for apprehension. He returned to Madinah in accordance with this Qur'anic injunction:

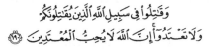

And fight in the Way of Allah against those who fight you, but do not transgress the limits. Truly, Allah likes not transgressors.

(Al Baqarah 2 :v 190)

During the Prophet's stay at Tabuk, he formulated many peace plans with the Christian states and tribes. The Christians were also asked to pay the defence tax in exchange for security of life and property. The following treaty was signed between Yuhannd Ibn Ruba, the Governor of Alya and the Prophet Muhammad:

"In the name of God, the Most Compassionate and the Most Merciful. This is a guarantee from God and Muhammad, the Messenger of Allah, Yuhannd Ibn Ruba and the people of Ayla, for their ships and their caravans by land and sea. They and all that are with them, men of Syria and those of Yemen and seamen, all have the protection of Allah and that of His Messenger. Whosoever contravenes this treaty, his wealth shall not save him, it shall be for the fair price of him that takes it. Now it should not be unlawful to hinder the men of Ayla from any springs which they have been in the habit of frequenting, nor from any journey they desire to make, whether by sea or by land."

Potential Murderers are Forgiven

During the expedition, there were a number of hypocrites who decided to join the Muslim army. No one could suspect that there would be an enemy from within the army. Using this as an advantage they had planned to kill the Prophet by pushing him off a high rocky passage that ran between the mountains at Aqabah.

However, Allah warned the Prophet of the hypocrites plans and thus the Prophet realised who the hypocrites were. The Prophet then related the plan to his companions who were so angry that they asked the Prophet to kill them all. But the Prophet characteristically forgave them.

Three Companions are Forgiven by Allah

There were three Muslims who had remained in Madinah and had not participated in the expedition. This was not due to ill-health or poverty, but due to human weakness. As a punishment, these three people were excluded from the life of the community. No one was to have any contact with them. This left them isolated and depressed. They then, of their own accord, repented sincerely to Allah and showed it through their deeds that there loyalty to Allah and His Messenger was unshaken. Allah, the Most Merciful forgave them for their disobedient actions. The Qur'an says:

وَعَلَى الثَّلَثَةِ الَّذِينَ خُلِّفُوا حَتَّى إِذَا ضَاقَتْ عَلَيْهِمُ الْأَرْضُ بِمَا رَحُبَتْ وَضَاقَتْ عَلَيْهِمْ أَنفُسُهُمْ وَظَنُّوا أَن لَّا مَلْجَأَ مِنَ اللَّهِ إِلَّا إِلَيْهِ ثُمَّ تَابَ عَلَيْهِمْ لِيَتُوبُوا إِنَّ اللَّهَ هُوَ التَّوَّابُ الرَّحِيمُ ﴿١١٨﴾

And (He did forgive also) the three [who did not join the Tabuk expedition (whom the Prophet)] left (i.e. he did not give his judgement in their case, and their cases were suspended for Allah's Decision) till for them the earth, vast as it is, was straitened and their own selves were straitened to them, and they perceived that there is no fleeing from Allah, and no refuge but with Him. Then, He accepted their repentance, that they might repent. Verily, Allah is the One Who accepts repentance, Most Merciful.

(At Tauba 9 :v 118)

Types of Men the Prophet Dealt With

During this expedition there were three categories of men, besides the sincere Muslims, whom the Prophet had to deal with. Firstly, he had to deal with the hypocrites:

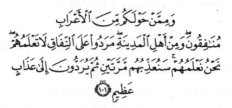

And among the Bedouins round about you, some are hypocrites, and so are some among you the people of Al-Madinah, they exaggerate and persist in hypocrisy, you know them not, We know them. We shall punish them twice, and thereafter they shall be brought back to a great (horrible) torment.

(At Tauba 9 :v 101)

The second type of men comprised of those Muslims who were honest in their faith but under the influence of human weakness had failed to carry out the orders of Allah. However, they sought forgiveness and Allah forgave them:

وَءَاخَرُونَ ٱعْتَرَفُوا بِذُنُوبِهِمْ خَلَطُوا عَمَلًا صَلِحًا
وَءَاخَرَ سَيِّئًا عَسَى ٱللَّهُ أَن يَتُوبَ عَلَيْهِمْ إِنَّ ٱللَّهَ غَفُورٌ رَّحِيمٌ ﴿١٠٢﴾

And (there are) others who have acknowledged their sins, they have mixed a deed that was righteous with another that was evil. Perhaps Allah will turn unto them in forgiveness. Surely, Allah is Oft-Forgiving , Most Merciful.

(At Tauba-9:v 102)

The third category included such people whose cases were doubtful cases and will be judged later by Allah:

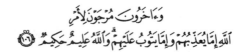

And others await Allah's Decree, whether He will punish them or will forgive them. And Allah is All Knowing, All Wise.

(At Tauba 9 :v 106)

The Mosque of the Hypocrites

The first mosque of Islam was built in Quba after the hijra of Prophet Muhammad. Later on, the hypocrites of the tribe of Banu Ghanam built an opposition mosque at Quba, pretending to advance the cause of Islam. In reality, they were conspiring against Islam from within the mosque. They tried to change the Qur'an by adding and deleting words and sentences but failed. To hide their evil activities, they invited the Prophet to come and pray in the mosque. But when the Prophet was about to go to the Mosque, the following verses were revealed:

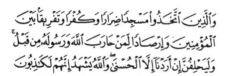

And as for those who put up a mosque by way of harming and disbelief, and to disunite the believers, and as an outpost for those who warred against Allah and His Messenger aforetime, they will indeed swear that their intention is nothing but good. Allah bears Witness that they are certainly liars.

(At Tauba 9 :v 107)

The mosque was then demolished and the hypocrites fled from the area. They received support only from their chief - Abdullah Ibn Ubayy.

Angel of Death Visits Abdullah Ibn Ubayy

Two months after the return of the Muslim army from Tabuk, the leader of the hypocrites, Abdullah Ibn Ubayy died. His son, who was a Muslim came to the Prophet and requested him to conduct the burial.

When the Prophet started praying over the body of Abdullah, Umar Ibn Al Khattab objected by saying: "O Prophet! Will you pray over one of the enemies of Allah?" The Prophet replied: "I have been given the choice, for Allah says:

$$\text{ٱسۡتَغۡفِرۡ لَهُمۡ أَوۡ لَا تَسۡتَغۡفِرۡ لَهُمۡ إِن تَسۡتَغۡفِرۡ لَهُمۡ سَبۡعِينَ مَرَّةً}$$
$$\text{فَلَن يَغۡفِرَ ٱللَّهُ لَهُمۡ ذَٰلِكَ بِأَنَّهُمۡ كَفَرُواْ بِٱللَّهِ وَرَسُولِهِۦ}$$
$$\text{وَٱللَّهُ لَا يَهۡدِى ٱلۡقَوۡمَ ٱلۡفَٰسِقِينَ ﴿٨٠﴾}$$

Whether you ask forgiveness for them (hypocrites) or ask not forgiveness for them (and even) if you ask seventy times for their forgiveness, Allah will not forgive them, because they have disbelieved in Allah and His Messenger. And Allah guides not those people who are Fasiqun (rebellious, disobedient to Allah).
(At Tauba 9 :v 80)

The Prophet even added: "If I knew that if I exceeded seventy times, Allah will forgive them then I would have done so." He then walked to the funeral procession and stood by the grave until the procession was over.

Umar later recalls: "I was amazed at my boldness with the Prophet, but soon after the following verses were revealed:

وَلَا تُصَلِّ عَلَىٰٓ أَحَدٍ مِّنْهُم مَّاتَ أَبَدًا وَلَا تَقُمْ

عَلَىٰ قَبْرِهِۦٓ إِنَّهُمْ كَفَرُوا۟ بِٱللَّهِ وَرَسُولِهِۦ وَمَاتُوا۟ وَهُمْ فَٰسِقُونَ ﴿٨٤﴾

And never pray (funeral prayer) for any of them (hypocrites) who dies, nor stand at his grave. Certainly they disbelieved in Allah and His Messenger, and died while they were Fasiqun (rebellious, disobedient to Allah and His Messenger."

(At Tauba 9: v 84)

This was the first and last time that the Prophet prayed over a hypocrite.

THE YEAR OF DELEGATIONS

Towards the end of the ninth and throughout the tenth year after Hijrah, delegations from various tribes kept pouring into Madinah. One of the major reason for this was the courage shown by the Muslims at Tabuk.

Urwa Ibn Mas'ud Embraces Islam

Urwa Ibn Mas'ud al Thaqafi was one of the main leaders of Thaqif, the tribe who lived in Taif. When the Muslims besieged Taif in the Battle of Hunayn, Urwa was still at Hudaybiya. He had remained there after the negotiations with the Muslims concerning the Hudaybiya Treaty. On his return, he went to Prophet Muhammad and embraced Islam. The conduct of the Prophet at the negotiations, and after it, had impressed him.

Upon embracing Islam his foremost concern thereafter was to see his own people and persuade them to follow the Straight Path *(As Siratul Mustaqim)*. The Prophet, from his own experience of dealing with the people of Taif, feared that they would kill Urwa and thus hesitated to give permission. But Urwa, full of the new spirit and faith assured the Prophet by saying: "I am dearer to them than the apple of their eye." Eventually the Prophet gave his permission.

Reaching Taif, Urwa summoned all of his people together and invited them to accept Islam. They listened but asked him to grant them permission to think the matter over. The next day Urwa woke up and sounded the Adhan for the dawn prayer. Instantly some

222

members of the tribe gathered around his house and shot arrows at him from every direction until he fell down. Just before his last breath, they asked him: "What do you think about your death?" He answered: "This is a gift with which Allah has honoured me and a martyrdom which Allah has led me to." These dying words of Urwa, later had a great effect upon the listeners.

Deputation from Taif

Realising the seriousness of the situation and the hostile reaction by other Arab tribes, a deputation was sent to Madinah to ask for forgiveness.

Prophet Muhammad greeted them gladly and accommodated them by the mosque. The people of the deputation were impressed by the beautiful recitation and message of the Qur'an and by the excellent conduct of the Muslims towards them, especially the Prophet.

They expressed their willingness to enter Islam. However, they asked for certain concessions. Firstly they asked that no check should be imposed on their lending money at interest. The Prophet did not agree, as interest is completely forbidden in Islam. The Qur'an says:

يَٰٓأَيُّهَا ٱلَّذِينَ ءَامَنُوا۟ ٱتَّقُوا۟ ٱللَّهَ وَذَرُوا۟ مَا بَقِيَ مِنَ ٱلرِّبَوٰٓا۟ إِن كُنتُم مُّؤۡمِنِينَ ۝

O you who believe! Be afraid of Allah and give up
what remains (due to you) from Riba (usury) (from now
onward), if you are (really) believers.
(Al-Baqarah 2 v : 278)

They also demanded that they should be permitted to drink alcohol. Again the Prophet refused the demand and recited these Qur'anic verses:

يَـٰٓأَيُّهَا ٱلَّذِينَ ءَامَنُوٓاْ إِنَّمَا ٱلۡخَمۡرُ وَٱلۡمَيۡسِرُ وَٱلۡأَنصَابُ وَٱلۡأَزۡلَـٰمُ رِجۡسٌ
مِّنۡ عَمَلِ ٱلشَّيۡطَـٰنِ فَٱجۡتَنِبُوهُ لَعَلَّكُمۡ تُفۡلِحُونَ ﴿٩٠﴾

O you who believe! Intoxicants (all kind of alcoholic drinks), gambling, Al-
Ansab and Al-Azlam (arrows for seeking luck or decision) are on abomination
of satan's handiwork. So avoid (strictly all) that
(abomination) in order that you may be successful.
(Al Ma'idah 5 : v 90)

They further asked as to what would be done to their goddess - al Lat. The Prophet's reply was: "Destroy her!" Some of them were bewildered while others expressed a fear that if the idol knew of their intention it would kill the inhabitants of the city. They begged that the idol be spared for some time. Firstly, they asked for three years, then two, then one and finally one month. Prophet Muhammad refused to except such nonsense. In a final attempt they asked that they should not be given the task of breaking al Lat and that they should be exempted from the five daily prayers. The latter request was rejected but the former was accepted. Concerning the prayers the Prophet said: "There is no good in religion without prayer." The Qur'an says :

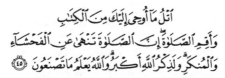

اتۡلُ مَآ أُوحِىَ إِلَيۡكَ مِنَ ٱلۡكِتَـٰبِ
وَأَقِمِ ٱلصَّلَوٰةَۖ إِنَّ ٱلصَّلَوٰةَ تَنۡهَىٰ عَنِ ٱلۡفَحۡشَآءِ
وَٱلۡمُنكَرِۗ وَلَذِكۡرُ ٱللَّهِ أَكۡبَرُۗ وَٱللَّهُ يَعۡلَمُ مَا تَصۡنَعُونَ ﴿٤٥﴾

Recite (O Muhammad) what has been revealed to you of the Book (the
Qur'an), and offer prayers perfectly (Iqamat-as-Salat). Verily prayer prevents

from Al Fahsha (i.e. great sins of every kind) and Al Munkar (i.e. disbelief, polytheism) and the praising of (you by) Allah (in front of the angels) is greater indeed (than your praising of Allah in prayers, etc.).
And Allah knows what you do.
(Al Ankabut 29 : v 45)

Abu Sufyan and Al Mughira were sent to break the idols. Sounds of the women of Taif wailing could be heard everywhere as the idols were destroyed. In agreement with the Prophet, the money in the temple of the idols was used to pay off a debt of Urwa Ibn Masud.

The deputation remained in Madinah until the end of Ramadhan and returned to Taif with their appointed teacher: Uthman Ibn Abu Al Aas. Not long after, the whole city of Taif came into the fold of Islam.

Abu Bakr Leads the Pilgrimage

The year went by and it was time for the pilgrimage to Makkah. This time the Prophet did not go but sent a caravan under the leadership of Abu Bakr.

After Abu Bakr had left, the holy verses came down saying that no polytheist should enter the House of Allah after that year. They were to be given four months in which they had to return to their land. If their relationship with the Muslims was to be improved, then they should forsake the idols and enter Islam, otherwise they should expect war. But those tribes who had agreements or treaties with the Prophet were to be treated according to the terms of the treaty until it expired.

Ali Ibn Abu Talib was sent after Abu Bakr with these new verses. The Muslims and the polytheists were informed of the verses. The house of Allah was now purely used for the worship of Allah.

Islam had now spread throughout the Peninsula. It's supremacy was fully established. Deputation from all quarters began to pour into Islam. The sound of war had almost died away. Once the Prophet sent Mu'adh to Yemen to teach people the Deen of Islam. He was given the following guidelines and principles:

'Make things easy and do not complicate them. Deal gently with people and show no harshness towards them. You are going to one of the People of the Book who will ask you what is the key to Paradise. Explain to them that the way to paradise is to testify that there is no God but Allah, He is One and Has no partner.'

The Prophet's Last Pilgrimage

Prophet Muhammad had successfully completed his mission. His duty was to make Islam supreme over all other systems of life. As the Qur'an says:

هُوَ ٱلَّذِىٓ أَرْسَلَ رَسُولَهُۥ بِٱلْهُدَىٰ وَدِينِ ٱلْحَقِّ لِيُظْهِرَهُۥ عَلَى ٱلدِّينِ كُلِّهِۦ وَلَوْ كَرِهَ ٱلْمُشْرِكُونَ ۞

He it is Who sent His Messenger (Muhammad) with Guidance and the
Religion of Truth (Islamic Monotheism) to make it victorious over all (other)
religions even though the 'Mushrikun' (polytheists, pagans, idolaters
and disbelievers in the Oneness of Allah and in His Messenger) hate (it).
(As Saff 61 : v 9)

The great change he brought within the short space of less than a quarter of a century, has no parallel in the history of the world. There is not a single reformer who has entirely changed the lives of a whole nation in such a short span of time. For twenty three long years he worked hard to make the rule of Allah supreme over any other rule. In these twenty three years, there was an all round transformation; no trace of an idol was left in Arabia. He had fulfilled his duty of calling people to worship Allah alone. He had formed a society based on the worship of Allah and total obedience to Him based on the principles of Tawhid, belief in Risalah and a firm conviction in the Akhirah (life after death). He had given the Arabs and non-Arabs light and had inspired them with belief in Allah. He gave unity of thought and action and created a strong brotherhood.

The month of Pilgrimage came again as the year passed. Prophet Muhammad was now in the sixty third year of his life. He decided to make the pilgrimage himself. Thousands of people flocked from all over the Peninsula upon hearing the news that Prophet Muhammad would also be at Makkah. All together there were nearly one hundred thousand (100,000) people (according to other sources one hundred and twenty thousand (120,000)). In this pilgrimage the wives of the Prophet accompanied him, contrary to all preceding travels and pilgrimages.

The pilgrimage, otherwise known as Hajj, was carried out. The Muslims circled the Ka'bah seven times, offered two Rakats of prayer at the 'Station of Ibrahim' and climbed the Mount of Safa.

On the 9th of Dhil Hijjah, in the 10th year of Hijrah, after the morning prayer, the Prophet went to Arafat and delivered the following farewell speech. The occasion was a memorable one; men, women and children from all walks of life, the rich and the poor were eager, attentive and waiting to listen to the Prophet. The Prophet addressed the gathering in such slow, clear sentences that every word rang like a silver bell. As each sentence was completed it was repeated aloud in various parts of the gathering so that it could reach the remotest corner of the vast assembly. The Prophet appointed Rabia Ibn Umayya to repeat after him to the people, part by part, exactly as he had said it.

THE FAREWELL SPEECH

O People! Listen to my words carefully, for I do not know whether I shall meet you again on such an occasion in the future.

O People! Your lives and property shall be inviolate until you meet your Lord. Sacred to you is the life and property of others. Remember that you will indeed meet your Lord, and He will indeed reckon your deeds. Thus do I warn you. Whoever of you is keeping a trust of someone else shall return that trust to its rightful owner. All interest obligation shall henceforth be waived. Your capital, however, is yours to keep. You will neither inflict or suffer inequity. Allah has forbidden interest, and I cancel the dues of interest payable to my uncle Al Abbas Ibn Abdul Muttalib.

O People! The devil has lost all hope of ever being worshipped in this land of yours. Nevertheless, he will try to mislead you in smaller matters. Beware of him, therefore, for the safety of your Deen.

O People! Tampering with the calendar is evidence of great unbelief and confirms the unbelievers in their misguidance. They indulge in it one year and forbid it the next in order to make permissible that which Allah forbade, and to forbid that which Allah has made permissible. The pattern according to which the time is reckoned is always the same. With Allah, the months are twelve in number. Four of them are holy. Three of these are successive and one occurs singly between the months of Jumada and Sha'ban.

O Man! Your wives have a certain rights over you and you have certain rights over them. It is your right that they do not fraternize with anyone of whom you do not approve of and that they do not commit adultery. But if they do fraternize with anyone of whom you disapprove, Allah has permitted you to isolate them within their homes and chastise them without cruelty. Treat them well and be kind to them, for they are your partners and committed helpers. You have taken them only as a trust from Allah and you have their enjoyment only by His permission.

O People! Listen carefully, All believers are brothers. The Muslims constitute one brotherhood. You are not allowed to take anything belonging to another Muslim unless he gives it to you willingly. Do not, therefore, do injustice to your own selves.

O People! None is higher than the other unless he is higher in obedience to Allah. No Arab is superior to a non Arab except in piety.

O People! Ponder over my words which I convey to you. I am leaving with you the Book of Allah (Qur'an) and the Sunnah of His Prophet. If you follow them you will never go astray.

O People! Be mindful of those who work under you. Feed and clothe them as you clothe yourselves.

O People! No Prophet or Messenger will come after me. Worship Allah and offer salah, observe sawm and pay zakah.

He ended by saying: "Be my witness O Allah, that I have conveyed

Your message to Your people?" And the people responded to this by saying: "Yes, you have (conveyed the message) Allah be Witness."

The Last Revelation

When the Prophet finished his speech, he dismounted from his camel and waited until noon, and then performed both the noon and the mid afternoon prayers (Zuhr and Asr). He then mounted back on his camel and went to Al-Shakharat. It was here that he recited the last revelation revealed unto him:

$$\text{ٱلْيَوْمَ يَئِسَ ٱلَّذِينَ كَفَرُواْ مِن دِينِكُمْ}$$
$$\text{فَلَا تَخْشَوْهُمْ وَٱخْشَوْنِ ٱلْيَوْمَ أَكْمَلْتُ لَكُمْ دِينَكُمْ وَأَتْمَمْتُ}$$
$$\text{عَلَيْكُمْ نِعْمَتِى وَرَضِيتُ لَكُمُ ٱلْإِسْلَٰمَ دِينًا}$$

This day, those who disbelieved have given up all hope of your religion, so fear them not, but fear Me. This day I have perfected your religion for you, completed My favour upon you and have chosen Islam as your Deen.

(Al Maidah 5 : v 3)

When Abu Bakr heard this verse, he realised that with the completion of the divine messages, the Prophet's life was soon to come to a close. He could feel that this was the end. Completion of the mission implied the Prophet's departure from this world.

The Prophet left Arafat and spent the night at Muzdalifah, then in the morning moved onto Al Ashr Al Haram. From there he went back to Mina and threw pebbles against the symbol of Shaitan (devil). When he reached his tent he sacrificed sixty three (63) camels, one for each year of his life. The Prophet then shaved his head and declared his pilgrimage complete. This pilgrimage is known as the 'Farewell Pilgrimage' or 'Pilgrimage of Annunciation' or 'Pilgrimage of Islam'.

Now that all the Arabs had united in this 'Farewell Pilgrimage' the Arabian Peninsula became secure in its entirety. Indeed there was no reason for any Arab kings and princes to withdraw or to violate their loyalty to the Prophet or to Islam. Under no other regime did they enjoy more power and internal autonomy than under that of the Prophet.

Prophet Muhammad, in the last year of his life, spent most of the time in Madinah. He settled the organisation of the provinces and tribal communities which had adopted Islam and had become component parts of the Islamic State. Officials were sent to the provinces and to various tribes for the purpose of teaching the people the principles and practicalities of Islam and also to administrate justice according to the Qur'an and Sunnah.

False Prophets

Prophet Muhammad paid little attention to those certain individuals who claimed to be Prophets. He had concentrated all his efforts on assembling an army to encounter movements of the Roman Troops on the northern border.

Certain individuals from certain tribes, had the feeling that if a man like Prophet Muhammad, a man from the Quraish, could have power over them, why do they not claim to be Prophets and they too would have power, pride and glory. Tulaybah, for instance, the leader of Banu Asad and one of the greatest war heroes claimed that he was a Prophet. The 'proof' of his prophethood was his true prophesying about the exact location of water when his people were once lost in the desert and almost died of thirst. But he remained afraid of contradicting Prophet Muhammad and therefore rebelled only after the Prophet's death. However, he repented and henceforth led a virtuous life.

There were also individuals such as Musaylamah and Al-Aswad Al Ansi. The former sent a message saying : "I too am a Prophet like you. To us belong half of the earth and to Quraish belongs the other half, if Quraish were only just." The Prophet replied: "The earth belongs to none but Allah, and Allah grants to whomsoever He chooses among His worthy and righteous servants. Peace belongs to the Rightly Guided."

Aswad Al Ansi, the Governor of Yemen began to practice magic and to call people to believe in him until he had a measure of strength. He then marched to South Yemen and expelled the Governors who were appointed by the Prophet. He marched onto Najran, killed its Governor, married the widow of the dead Governor and brought the whole area of Najran under his control. Such was the domination of Islam and power of the Prophet that this incident did not concern him the slightest. He simply sent a message to his Governors in Yemen to end Al Aswad's rule. Consequently the regime was abolished and dismantled. As for Aswad, he was killed by his own wife who decided to take revenge for the loss of her first husband.

Preparations Against Rome

The Prophet was convinced that Muslim power at the northern border with Al Sham should be firmly established if those who had been expelled from the Peninsula and who had emigrated to Palestine, were not to return and attack again.

Therefore, on their return from the 'Farewell Pilgrimage' a large army was mobilised and was commanded to march on Al Sham. Included in that army were Abu Bakr and Umar. But the Prophet Muhammad appointed Usamah Ibn Zayd as the commander of the army.

Usamah was then a young man of hardly twenty years of age. His appointment was to honour the name of his father who had been killed while commanding at the battle of Mutah. Such an appointment was also sure to stir within the blood of the youth the greatest determination and bravery. It was also meant as an example for the youth of Islam to carry the burden of great responsibility. The Prophet commanded him to fight the enemy in the early hours of dawn and when Allah granted him victory, to return back to Madinah.

THE PROPHET FALLS ILL

Usamah and his army were ready to set forth, but news reached them that the Prophet had become seriously ill and thus the preparations were brought to a halt. The love and the concern for the Prophet prevented them from undertaking a campaign which the Prophet himself had ordered.

The Prophet had never been seriously ill before. Nothing had adversely affected his health throughout his life except from eating a bite of poisoned lamb. He always ate little and satisfied himself with the very basic necessities: dry bread, a few dates or a little milk, and sometimes he ate honey. His clothes and house were always perfectly clean. Not only did he make sure that the duties of ablution were perfectly carried out all the time, but he even used to say: "Were it not for my fear of imposing hardship on my people, I would have made it a duty for them to brush their teeth five times a day." All these aspects of his character protected him against disease and gave him good health.

It was natural for his friends and companions to become concerned and anxious. They had never seen the Prophet ill before.

The Prophet Visits the Graves

On the first day of his illness, when he was able to move about the Prophet went to visit the graves of Baqi Al Gharqad accompanied by Abu Muwayhibah, his servant. The Prophet stood between the graves and said: "Peace unto to you, people of the graves, and joy for what you are and what people are in, for temptation, like dark patches of the night come one after the other." Abu Muwayhibah relates that the Prophet said to him as they were going out of Baqi Al Gharqad: "O Abu Muwayhibah, I have been given the choice of this world and eternity in it as well as Paradise after it or meeting with my Lord and Paradise now." Abu Muwayhibah suggested that he should accept both options, but the Prophet had already decided: "I have chosen the meeting with my Lord and Paradise now."

The next day he visited his relations and went to visit his wives. He found A'ishah complaining of a headache: "Woe my head." The Prophet answered: "But rather, O A'ishah, woe my head!" The pain was not strong enough to prevent him talking kindly to his wives and joking with them. He was in the house of Maymunah when the pain returned with a stronger force. He asked their (his wives) permission to be nursed in the house of A'ishah. They all agreed. He then moved out of Maymunah's house, his body wrapped, leaning on Ali Ibn Abu Talib on one side and on Al Abbas, his uncle, on the other. His legs could hardly carry him.

When the attacks of fever subsided, the Prophet walked to the mosque to lead the prayers. He could hear the companions gossiping about his appointment of a very young man to command an army which consisted of men of such calibre as Abu Bakr and Umar. Despite the pain, he felt it necessary to address the people on that subject. He went out and addressed the people.

Relationship With Abu Bakr

Standing on the pulpit he said: "O Men! Carry out the expedition under Usamah. Your complaint against his generalship is of the same kind as your complaint against the generalship of his father before him. By Allah! Usamah is as fit for the generalship as was his father." The Prophet stopped for a while and resumed by saying: "A slave of Allah who was asked to choose between this world and the eternal life has chosen the eternal with Allah." Again it was only Abu Bakr who realised the underlying meaning and would have burst into tears had not the Prophet signalled to him to control his tears. The Prophet was concerned that the others might be affected emotionally and psychologically.

Later, the Prophet consoled Abu Bakr by saying: "I do not know of anyone whose companionship is dearer to me than yours. Of all the people of the world I would choose only Abu Bakr as a permanent friend and constant companion. His has been the friendship of true faith, and it will last until Allah brings us together again."

The following day Prophet Muhammad was too tired to lead the prayers and asked that Abu Bakr should lead the prayers. The Prophet's wife, A'ishah, insisted that her father's voice was too soft and that he would break down and cry, whenever he recited the Qur'an. But the Prophet did not change his opinion and thus Abu Bakr led the prayers.

On one occasion, Abu Bakr was absent so Umar led the prayers. As Umar's loud voice reached the ear of the Prophet, he asked: "Where is Abu Bakr? Allah and the believers do not agree that Abu Bakr be not the leader." From this saying, people were convinced that the Prophet Muhammad has indeed appointed Abu Bakr as his successor. Prophet Muhammad would not command them directly to let Abu Bakr be the Khalifah after him as the Qur'an decrees that the affairs of Muslims are settled by consultation among themselves; but suggested to them in different ways; by letting and wanting him to lead the prayers, by letting him lead the pilgrimage at Makkah and by praising him as the best companion he ever had.

Fatimah Cries, Fatimah Laughs

Soon after this the Prophet's pain increased. Fatimah, his only daughter, whom he loved very dearly, visited him everyday. One day he rose to greet her and asked her to sit beside him. He then whispered something twice, first making her cry then making her laugh. A'ishah was confused. It was after the Prophet's death that Fatimah explained to A'ishah that she had cried because the Prophet told her that he will be returned to Allah in this illness, then she laughed when he told her that she would be the first to join him. Fatimah died six months after the Prophet's death.

The Prophet Wishes to Write

One day while under a strong attack of fever and surrounded by his companions, he asked that a pen, ink and paper be brought to him. He said that he would dictate something for his followers benefit, assuring them that if they adhered to it, they would never go astray.

Some of them hurried to get the materials, but others among them thought that since the Prophet was extremely ill and they all ready had the Qur'an, no further writing was necessary. Umar was reported to have held this opinion. The people present disagreed amongst themselves. The Prophet asked them all to leave saying : "It does not befit you to disagree in my presence."

After the Prophet passed away, some expressed regrets at this lost opportunity. Ibn Abbas at the time said that the people would lose something important if they did not hasten to bring the writing materials, whereas Umar held firmly to his judgement which he based upon Allah's own estimate of the Qur'an:

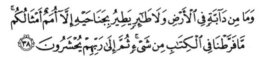

There is not a moving (living) creature on earth, nor a bird that flies with its two wings, but are communities like you. We have neglected nothing in the Book, then unto their Lord they shall be gathered.

(Al An'am 6 : v 38)

Disposing the Seven Dinars

At the beginning of his illness, the Prophet had seven dinars; he feared that he might die while some money was in his possession, thus he instructed his relatives to give the money to the poor. But due to their preoccupation with the Prophet's sickness they forgot. He asked them one day, what they had done with the seven dinars. When he heard that they still had the money he said: "What would Muhammad do if he met his Lord and this was with him?" The money was then distributed amongst the poor.

THE PROPHET PASSES AWAY

On the day that was to be the last day of his life, Prophet Muhammad slept a quiet sleep and felt better. He went out to the dawn prayer leaning on Ali and Abbas. The Muslims were happy and overjoyed to see the Prophet in a better state. Surely, they thought, he would recover to his former health. However the Prophet signalled to Abu Bakr to lead the prayer. After the prayer, which was to be his last prayer, he spoke to them collectively for the last time: "O men, the fire is ready. Subversive attacks are advancing like the waves of darkness. By Allah, I shall not be held responsible. I have never allowed anything but that which the Qur'an has made legitimate, and I have never forbidden that but which the Qur'an forbids." He also said: "After me, you will differ much. Whatever agrees with the Qur'an is from me; whatever differs from the Qur'an is not from me."

The Muslims were all optimistic after seeing the Prophet in a better condition of health. But this did not last for long; immediately after he spoke with them, the Prophet began to feel weaker and weaker. He knew that the time had come to meet his Lord. When the fever was at its peak, he put his hand in a bowl of water and wiped his forehead and said: "O Allah, help me bear the agonies of death." His last words were in answer to a question unheard by those around him: "Nay, the eternal companion in Paradise." The Prophet then passed away on the laps of his beloved wife A'ishah. It was the 12th of Rabiul Awwal in the 11th year of Hijrah.

Muslims Are Shocked

The Muslims at the mosque were taken by surprise by the sudden noise of crying, knowing the implication of it. Just a few hours ago they had seen the Prophet and were convinced that his health was improving, so much so that even Abu Bakr had sought permission to go to his house in the outskirts of Madinah to visit his wife. It was very hard for them to accept the reality, but what else were they to think?

Reaction of Umar Ibn Al Khattab

Upon receiving the news and hardly believing what his ears had heard, Umar Ibn Al Khattab stood with his sword unsheathed and announced that anyone who dared to say that Prophet Muhammad is dead would do so at the cost of his life. He further added: "Some hypocrites are pretending that the Prophet of Allah, has died. By Allah, I swear that he did not die: he has gone to join his Lord, just as Musa went before. Musa absented himself from his people on fourteen consecutive nights and returned to them after they declared him dead. By Allah, the Prophet will return just as Musa returned." Hearing this, some of the Muslims held a glimmer of hope. But it all diminished when Abu Bakr arrived.

This reaction by Umar was natural for his character. He had a very emotional, reactive and brave personality. It was unthinkable for him that the man who was Allah's Last Messenger, the man whom he spent the latter part of his life with, the man who transformed his life and the man who was a salvation unto mankind, could die.

Reaction of Abu Bakr

As soon as Abu Bakr heard the news, he returned from Al Sunh. He looked through the door of the mosque and saw Umar addressing the Muslims. He then went straight to the Prophet's body, uncovered his face and kissed him saying: "How good you were alive, and how good you look, even in death." Then he covered the face and went out to meet the people.

Umar was still proclaiming loudly that Prophet Muhammad had not died. When Abu Bakr reached Umar, he said to him: "Softly, O Umar! Keep silent!" But Umar would not stop talking. Abu Bakr made a sign to the people that he was going to address them. After praising Allah, Abu Bakr said: "He who worshipped Muhammad, let him know that Muhammad is dead. But he who worships Allah, let him know Allah is alive and never dies." He then recited the Qur'anic verse:

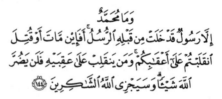

Muhammad is no more than a Messenger, and indeed (many) Messengers have passed away before him. If he dies or is killed, will you turn back on your heels (as disbelievers)? And he who turns back on his heels, not the least harm will he do to Allah, and Allah will give reward to those who are grateful.

(Al Imran 3 : v 144)

Abu Bakr, inspite of his intense grief, kept a cool head. He knew that the shock of Prophet Muhammad's death had been great, but the reaction might be even greater.

Umar soon realised the reality of the situation. He had invented the idea that the Prophet Muhammad would consult his Lord and then return to them as a shield for his own heart against the terrible reality. Umar fell down unconscious. The certainty that the Prophet of Allah was dead, shattered him.

Others were in no doubt, after hearing the Qur'anic verses, that the Prophet Muhammad had died. Tears of sorrow and grief began to flow from every one of them.

ABU BAKR BECOMES KHALIFAH

A dispute arose among the Muslims in answer to the obvious question; who was to become the successor of Prophet Muhammad? Who was to be the Khalifah? In fact this discussion arose and a Khalifah was nominated even before the burial of the Prophets body.

The Ansar had already gathered in the Court of Banu Saidah in order to decide the issue. Disputes arose amongst the Ansar and the Muhajirun. Both sides expressed their feelings to be the group of the man who would become Khalifah.

When Abu Bakr heard of this, he and Umar decided to go to Banu Saidah and settle the dispute. Abu Bakr tried his best to calm the matter and was successful. It was Umar who took the first step in the nomination of Khalifah. Abu Bakr had proposed that Umar Ibn Al Khattab or Abu Ubaydah Banu Al Jarrah were the most suitable candidates. But Umar reacted by saying: "O Abu Bakr, stretch out your hand and I will give you my oath of allegiance. Did not the Prophet himself command you to lead the Muslims in prayer? You, therefore are his successor. We elect you to this position. In electing you, we are electing the best of all those whom the Prophet of Allah loved and trusted." These words touched the hearts of everybody present. They recognised that it would have been the Prophet's wish that Abu Bakr be his successor. They themselves had witnessed the Prophet's insistence that Abu Bakr should lead the prayers even in his presence. The leader in the prayer, was also the leader of the community. Thus the dispute amongst the Ansar and Muhajirun was resolved and they all gave the oath of allegiance to him *(Al Bay'atul Khassah)*.

The next day, the majority of the Muslims elected and gave their consent to Abu Bakr becoming the Khalifah *(Al Bay'atul Aammah)*. Upon nomination Abu Bakr rose and delivered a speech, which in itself proves that he was the person to lead the Muslims:

'O people I have been chosen by you as your leader even though I am not better than any of you. If I do any good in my job help me. If I do wrong, correct me. Truth is honesty and falseness is treason. The weak among you are the powerful in my eyes until I restore their lost rights. The strong among you shall be the weak in my eyes, as long as I do not take away from them what is due to others. If people give up striving for the cause of Allah (Jihad fi Sabilillah) he will send down disgrace on them. If people become evil-doers, Allah will send down calamities upon them. Obey me as long as I obey Allah and His Prophet. But if I disobey Allah's command or His Prophet then disobey me."

Burial of the Prophet

After the appointment of the Khalifah, attention was drawn to the burial of the Prophet. There was a small disagreement as to where the Prophet should be buried. Some of the Muhajirun advised that the Prophet be buried in Makkah since it was his birth place. Others advised that he ought to be buried in Jerusalem where the Prophets were buried before him. Both of these were rejected and it was decided that the Prophet would be buried in Madinah. Once this was decided, a suitable place was needed to bury the Prophet.

Again there was a difference of opinion. Some expressed the opinion that the most suitable place would be in the mosque, on the spot of the pulpit he used. This was rejected, especially after A'ishah related that the Prophet, in his last days, used to curse the people who had taken the graves of their Prophet as places of worship. The issue was solved by the newly appointed Khalifah who related that he had heard the Prophet Muhammad say that Prophets should be buried wherever they die. Everybody accepted this decision and thus the Prophet of Allah, the last Messenger on earth was buried on the spot he died: in the house of A'ishah.

His body was washed and laid out. The body was then lowered into the grave, the bottom of which had been covered with the Prophet's mantle. This burial marked an end to an astonishing era and a beginning of another wonderful period in the history of Islam.

Appendix

AFTERWORD

This was just a brief description of the life and personality of the Final Messenger of Allah. We have seen how the Prophet struggled and suffered in fulfilling the purpose of his mission - the dominance of Islam over all other ways of life. He initiated an Islamic Movement through which people were gathered, organised and trained. The jama'ah was strengthened by unity of thought, strategic planning and mutual love and respect for one another. The tarbiyyah was a comprehensive guided tarbiyyah - it was ideological as well was practica,l and it was physical as well as spiritual. The vision of the Movement was Jannah and everything centred around this vision. The goal of the Movement was attaining the pleasure of Allah. The methodology of the Movement was based on *rabbaniyyah* (godliness), *waqi'iyah* (understanding the reality), *shumuliyyah* (comprehensiveness), *awlawiyyatul amal* (prioritising the work) and *tadarruj* (gradualness).

The Prophet's Islamic Movement was successful in attaining its aims and objectives. All over the Arabian Peninsula, Islam had become the ruling authority in all spheres of life. Supremacy and Sovereignty was only for Allah. The dominance of Islam continued even after the Prophet's death. The phenomena of Islam recognised no geographical border or cultural diversity; hence Islam prevailed in the south of Africa as it prevailed in the west of Spain. This Rule of Islam continued, having its high points and low points, until the beginning of the present century. In 1924 the Islamic Khilafah was officially destroyed and demolished by Mustapha Kamal Ataturk in Turkey.

Thus, we find ourselves in the same situation in which the Prophet found himself in; the main difference being the presence of millions of Muslims. Despite this number, and despite the numerous groups and movements that have arisen to re-establish the Khilafah, the Muslims as yet, live without a Khilafah and a Khalifah. It would not be an exaggeration to say that the Muslim Ummah is currently passing through its worst period in history. On the one hand the Muslim Ummah has never been weak before as it is today and on the other, the enemies of Islam have never been as strong before as they are today. What is more worrying is that, in the past, the enemies of Islam were distinctive and known to the Muslims, but today we do not even know who our real enemies are.

But not to despair! This is the Sunnah of Allah. It is He Who gives the power and authority to whom He Wishes; and takes away the power and authority from who He Wishes [Surah Al Imran 3: 26]. Allah also says in the Qur'an that He does not change the condition of people until they change what is in within themselves [Surah Ar R'ad 13:11].

He further promises that He will grant power and authority, as he has granted it to others before, but on two conditions - Iman (belief) and A-male Salih (righteous actions) [Surah Nur 24:55].

Mankind is on the verge of entering the 21st Century. With sound Iman, sincere intentions, deep knowledge, righteous actions, comprehensive understanding, guided tarbiyyah, patience and sacrifice, mutual co-operation, strategic thinking and planning and with the Help of Allah, the Muslims (the youth under the guidance of the elders) of the 21st Century will restore to the world that long awaited leadership - Insha Allah. A leadership that will bring humanity out from its present darkness to the light of Islam. A leadership that will not only advocate but also establish justice and equality. A leadership that will offer hope for humanity and give it direction. A leadership that will bring success in this world and in the Hereafter.

We pray to Allah to make our present days better than our past days, and to grant us better days in the future. Ameen.

SEERAH AT A GLANCE

Life in Makkah

Birth	Monday, 22nd April, 571 CE
	12 Rabiul Awwal
	Fifty days after the 'event of the elephants'
	Father Abdullah died before the Prophet's birth
4 months	First given to Thuwaybah to nurse and then to Halima
At age 6yrs	Death of his mother Aminah
8	Death of his grandfather Abdul Muttalib
12	First business trip to Syria
15	Participation in Battle of Al Fujjar
16	Member of Hilful Fudhul
24	Second business trip to Syria
25	Marriage to Khadijah
35	Settlement of Al Hajarul Aswad dispute
40	Prophethood in 611 CE

1st year of Prophethood

1st - 3rd year	Fajr and Asr prayers; 2 Rakah each
	Secret stage of Da'wah
	Approximatrly 40 people accept Islam
	Centre: Darul Arqam Al Makhzumi
3rd year	Beginning of open stage of Da'wah from Mount Safa
3rd - 5th year	Ridicule, Propaganda and Persecution
	Attempts at Compromise

5th year	Migration of Muslims to Abyssinia
6th year	Hamzah and Umar Ibn Al Khattab accept Islam
7th - 9th year	Boycott and confinement by the Quraish at Shibi Abu Talib
10th year	Year of Sorrow
	Death of his uncle Abu Talib and his wife Khadijah
	Visit to Taif
	Mi'raj, 27 Rajab
	Five times daily prayer made obligatory
11th year	First Pledge of Al Aqabah
12th year	Second Pledge of Al Aqabah
13th year	Hijrah to Madinah, 27 Safar

Life in Madinah

Hijrah	Makkah to Cave Thawr to arrival at Quba
1st year of Hijrah	Arrival at Madinah, Friday
	Construction of the Mosque
	Establishment of First Islamic State
	As Sahifah: First constitution of the world
	Establishment of Salah in congregation
	Marriage to Ayesha
2nd Hijrah	Jihad ordained: 12th of Safar
	Adhan and the change of Qiblah
	Ramadhan and Zakah made obligatory
	Battle of Badr: 17 Ramadhan
	Siege of Banu Qainuqa
3rd Hijrah	First restriction on drinking wine revealed

		Battle of Uhud: 5 Shawwal
		First order regarding interest revealed
		Laws of inheritance revealed
		Laws about marriage and rights of women
4th	Hijrah	Order of Hijab for women
		Final prohibition of alcohol
		The Second Badr
5th	Hijrah	Laws about adultery and slander revealed
		Battle of the Trench
		Punishment of Banu Quraizah
6th	Hijrah	Treaty of Hudaybiya
		Khalid and Amr Ibn Al Aas accept Islam
7th	Hijrah	Letters to the rulers of the Persian and Roman Empires
		Battle of Khaibar
		Performance of postponed Umrah
		Laws about marriage and divorce revealed
8th	Hijrah	Battle of Mutah
		Conquest of Makkah: 20 Ramadhan
		Battle of Hunayn
		Siege of Taif
		Final order prohibiting interest revealed
9th	Hijrah	Battle of Tabuk
		Order of Jizyah (protection tax on minorities)
		Hajj made obligatory
10th	Hijrah	Farewell Address: 9 Dhul Hijjah
Death		12 Rabiul Awwal: 11th Hijrah 632 CE

A COLLECTION OF NON-MUSLIM VERDICTS ON PROPHET MUHAMMAD

1. "Muhammad was the soul of kindness, and his influence was left and never forgotten by those around him."

> Diwan Chand Sharma
> The Prophet of the East
> Calcutta, 1935. p122

2. "I wanted to know the best of the life of one who holds today undisputed sway over the hearts of millions. I became more than ever convinced that it was not the sword that won a place for Islam in those days in the scheme of life. It was the rigid simplicity, the utter self effacement of the prophet, the scrupulous regard for pledges, his intense devotion to his friends and followers, his intrepidity, his fearlessness, his absolute trust in God and in his own mission. These and not the sword carried everything before them and surmounted every obstacles."

> Mahatma Ghandhi
> Young India, 1922

3. "I doubt whether any man whose external conditions changed so much ever changed himself less to meet them."

> Rev. C. Bodley
> The Messenger
> London, 1953. p33

4. "People like Pasteur and Salk are leaders in the first sense. People like Ghandhi and Confucius, on one hand, and Alexander, Caesar

and Hitler on the other, are leaders in the second and perhaps the third sense. Jesus and Buddha belong in the third category alone. Perhaps the greatest leader of all times was Mohammed,who combined all three functions."

Professor Jules Masserman

5. "By a fortune absolutely unique in history. Mohammed is a threefold founder of a nation, of an empire, and of a religion."

Rev. R. Bosworth Smith,
Mohammed and Mohammedanism, 1946

6. "Muhammad is the most successful of all prophets and religious personalities."

Encyclopedia Britannica

7. "An honest man is the noblest work of God. Muhammad was more than honest. He was human to the marrow of his bones. Human sympathy, human race, human love was the music of his soul.Tto serve man, to elevate man, to purify man, to educate man, in a word, to humanise man - this was the object of his mission."

Professor Ramakrishna Rao

8. "If a man like Muhammad were to assume dictatorship of the modern world, he would succeed in solving its problems that would bring it the much needed peace and happiness. Europe is beginning to be enamoured of the creed of Muhammad. In the next century it may go further in recognising the utility of that creed in solving its problems. "

George Bernard Shaw

9. "I have studied him - the wonderful man - and in my opinion far from being an anti-Christ, he must be called the saviour of humanity."

George Bernard Shaw
The Genuine Islam

10. "Head of the state as well as the church, he was Caesar and Pope in one: but, he was Pope without the Pope's pretensions, and Caesar without the legions of Caesar, without a standing army, without a bodyguard, without a police force, without a fixed revenue."

Rev. R. Bosworth Smith

11. "If ever a man had the right to say that he ruled by a divine right, it was Muhammad, for he had all their powers without their support. He cared for not the dressings of power. The simplicity of his private life was in keeping with his public life."

Rev. R. Bosworth Smith

12. "In little more than a year he was actually the spiritual, nominal and temporal ruler of Medina, with his hands on the lever that was to shake the world."

John Austin
'Muhammad the Prophet of Allah' in Cassel's weekly
24th September 1927

13. "Muhammad was one of the most profoundly sincere and earnest spirits of any age or epoch. A man not only great but one of the greatest men that humanity has ever produced; great not only as a Prophet but as a patriot and as a spiritual builder who

constructed a great nation, a great empire and more even than all three - a great faith, true moreover because he was true to himself, to his people and above all to his God.

Mayor A G Leonard

14. "The league of nations founded by the Prophet of Islam put the principle of international unity and human brotherhood on such universal foundations as to show candle to other nations."

Professor Hurgronze

15. "Philosopher, Orator, Apostle, Legislator, Warrior, Conqueror of ideas, Restorer of national beliefs, of a cult without images; the founder of twenty terrestrial empires and of one spiritual empire, that is Muhammad..."

La Martine
Historia de La Turquie

16."As regards all standards by which human greatness may be measured, we may well ask, is there any man greater than he ?"

La Martine
Historia de La Turquie
Paris, 1854, vol 2 p276-277

17. "That his (Muhammad's) reforms enhanced the status of women in general is universally admitted."

H. A. Gibb
Mohammedanism
London, 1953. p33

18. "Four years after the death of Justinian AD 56, was born at Mecca, in Arabia the man who, of all men exercised the greatest influence upon the human race - Mohammed."

John William Draper
A History of the Intellectual Development of Europe
London, 1875, vol 1 p329-330

19. "It is impossible for anyone who studies the life and character of the great Prophet of Arabia, who knows how he taught and how he lived, to feel anything but reverence for that mighty Prophet, one of the great Messengers of the Supreme. And although in what I put to you I shall say many things which may be familiar to many yet I myself feel whenever I re-read them, a new way of admiration, a new reverence for that mighty Arabian teacher."

Annie Besant
The Life and Teachings of Muhammad
Madras, 1932. p4

20. "It is the unparalleled combination of secular and religious influence which I feel entitles Muhammad to be considered the most influential single figure in human history."

Michael H. Hart
The 100 : A ranking of the Most Influential Persons in History
America, 1978

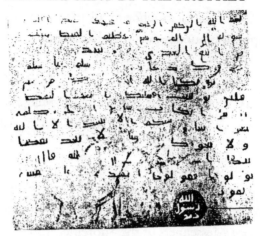

A copy of the letter sent to Muqawqis, Governor of Egypt,
inviting him to Islam from Muhammad the Messenger of Allah.

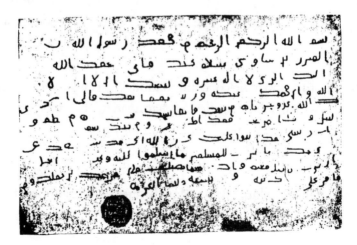

A copy of the letter sent to Al-Mundhir, Governor of Bahrain,
inviting him to Islam from Muhammad the Messenger of Allah

A copy of the letter sent to Chosroes Parvez, King of Persia,
inviting him to Islam from Muhammad the Messenger of Allah

A copy of the letter sent to Najashi, King of Abyssinia, inviting
him to Islam from Muhammad the Messenger of Allah

SELECTED REFERENCES

The author feels no need to list the numerous books that have been read and quoted during the course of writing this book. However, the main reference materials are mentioned below. It is mainly based upon the following books that most of the factual information about the Seerah had been derived.

Qur'an

1. Interpretation of the Meaning of the Noble Qur'an
Translators: Dr. Muhammad Hilali and Dr. Muhsin Khan

Classical Books

1. *Seerat ur Rasul-Allah*   Ibn Ishaq
2. *Seerat un Nabee*   Ibn Hisham
3. *Al Bidaya Wal Nihayah* Ibn Kathir
4. *Tarikh Al Tabari*   Imam Al Tabari
5. *Ash Shifa*   Qadi Iyad

Contemporary Books

1. *Fiqh us Seerah*   Shaykh Ramadhan Al Buti
2. *Fiqh us Seerah*   Shaykh Muhammad Al Ghazali
3. *Seerat un Nabee*   Maulana Shibli Numani
4. *Muhammad Rasul-Allah* Maulana Abul Hasan Ali Nadwi
5. *Seerate Sarware Alam*   Maulana Abul Ala Mawdudi
6. *Benefactor to Humanity* Allama Naeem Siddiqi
7. *Seerat ul Mustafa*   Maulana Idris Kandhalvi